ROBERT BURNS was born on 25th January, 1759, at Alloway in Ayrshire, and died on 21st July, 1796, at Dumfries.

His father was a working gardener from south of Stonehaven, in Kincardineshire. He was a hard-working man with high ideas about human worth and conduct. By precept and example, he had much to do with Robert's education and upbringing.

By modern standards, Robert had the sketchiest of education. But at an early age he was proficient in the three Rs and well grounded in the principles of Presbyterian theology. He read what he could lay his hands on and understood what he read.

The only mystery concerning Burns, whether in boyhood or manhood, is that of the quality of his genius.

He belongs to the company of the supremely great – Beethoven, Shakespeare, Rembrandt . . .

He could read and write and remember. He was surcharged with emotion, awareness, sensibility. And despite his background and foreground of poverty and hunger and never-ceasing toil, he could laugh. He relished the gift of life as few mortals have. He paid a terrible price for this quality of enjoyment; but he paid it gladly enough. He accepted the penalties imposed by necessity.

3

Early, too early for his growing, undernourished body, he was at the plough and executing the orra work about a poor, under-capitalised farm. He strained his heart; he became subject to bouts of rheumatic fever or something akin to that baffling ailment.

He laboured on Mount Oliphant. He laboured on Lochlea. When his father died there, prematurely worn out and exhausted (Burns was then twenty-four years of age) he, together with his brother Gilbert, rented the farm of Mossgiel near Mauchline.

Mossgiel was doomed to failure, not because Robert or Gilbert were bad farmers, but because they hadn't the necessary minimum of capital to work it economically.

But, brose-and-bannock toil apart, Robert Burns was a genius who expressed himself in poetry. As poet he could not be suppressed. As poet he triumphed. His was by no means an easy triumph – but then few triumphs of the first order are ever easy.

It was the nature of Robert Burns's experience that conditioned his poetry. He knew the nature of man and woman opposed to the bare elements of existence. His experience, if searing, was fundamental and therefore universal.

It is this supreme quality that makes Burns the first world-poet. Burns embraces all humanity. Humanity has, in turn, embraced him. So close (to give a random example) is he to Chinese thought and feeling that the

Chinese have suggested that he was of their race. French, Germans, Italians, Austrians, Russians, Americans, have claimed him as their own. The unco guid, the rigidly righteous, the Holy Willies, the Hornbooks, the Cotters, the Man made to Mourn, the Mouse – none of these is exclusive to eighteenth-century Ayrshire. They are universal and timeless.

Burns wrote of them for the most part in the Scottish dialect – a dialect of the great English tongue; and yet a dialect that generations of nobly-gifted Scots have raised to the dignity of a language in its own right.

We remain baffled to know *how* he did what he did. No academic analysis of his poems and songs in relation to their metre or their antecedents tells us anything of other than purely academic interest.

An understanding of his background, his foreground and his times is not without value. But it is mainly in relation to the dominating circumstances of his time, against which Burns and his contemporaries moved, that he can best be understood.

Basically, Burns was a humanitarian. Thus he was a libertarian and equalitarian. Actually, as his *Love and Liberty* shows, he was something more – and the world has yet to catch up on that something more.

Overall, his sympathies were for the poor, the oppressed; and his sympathy extended to the animal kingdom – to the mouse, the auld mare, the wounded hare. . . . He hated all manner of cruelty, oppression and the arrogance of privilege and mere wealth.

But many other worthy poets have had similar feelings. This in itself is not enough. Burns could look and laugh at a' that. His laughter, however is as broad as his humanity and there is no bitterness, no malice in his laughter. He laughs with life: never against it.

Burns is universal; but in his universality he is unique. There is no other poet like him. And thus, in a peculiar sense, he isn't a poet at all. He had no predecessors: he has had no disciples; and he is much too gigantic, too overflowing at too many points to be neatly, adequately or illuminatingly categorised, labelled and filed away.

Explain the mystery, the ramifications of human life, love, emotion and intellect and you can explain Robert Burns: not otherwise.

Burn's love for his fellowmen, for humanity, is all-embracing – and this despite the fact that his awareness is such that no other poet has shown such insight into the meanness, the cruelties and the follies of mankind. He is nothing of a sentimentalist.

He also loved women in the particular. He loved many women in his lifetime. Of his fifteen children, nine were born in 'lawful wedlock'. But in no sense was Burns a libertine. Of no other man is it recorded that he looked upon the children he fathered in or out of wedlock as his, and not the mother's, responsibility. Burns was supremely conscious of the glory of parenthood – legitimacy or illegitimacy were meaningless words to him: he spat the morality that begot them out of his mouth.

The supreme love of his life was Jean Armour, whom he married at the age of twenty-six. It was a supremely happy and altogether fortunate marriage, even if the early years were chequered by circumstances beyond the control of either.

In 1786, while at Mossgiel, and in anticipation of emigrating to the Indies, his first volume of poems and songs was published. It was an immediate success. He was read by high and low alike.

Instead of going to the Indies, he went to Edinburgh and within a few days was acclaimed as one of the wonders of the world.

A new and enlarged edition of his poems resulted. He toured Scotland in triumph – as Caledonia's Bard.

But he endured all this without affectation or illusion. His feet remained firmly on the earth. The pattern of life in Edinburgh or elsewhere in Scotland differed in no essential from the pattern of the small Ayrshire parish. The world of men revolves on the axis of the parish pump.

After Edinburgh, there remained the problem (as ever) of earning a living. He set up as a tenant-farmer in Ellisland at Dumfries. Again he was without sufficient capital to see him over the inevitable rainy day.

So he entered the Excise service as a common gauger at £50 a year. In a short space of time he rose to a foot-walk in Dumfries at £70 a year. He was an excellent farmer: he made a good Exciseman.

But Burns could not suppress the poet in him. By having some good friends 'in court' he escaped being sent to Botany Bay for treason, sedition and sympathy with the British Reform movement (a by-product of the French Revolution). *Scots Wha hae,* for example, had to be published anonymously. So savage was reaction in the saddle that William Blake observed that to defend the Bible would cost a man his life.

His public work continued, however, and he laboured (unpaid) to supply 'words and music' for the collections of James Johnson and George Thomson. In a very real sense Burns was as great a musician as he was a poet.

He dedicated himself to rescuing from oblivion and neglect hundreds of songs without words – or with fragmentary or unsuitable words. He knew that a song without words dies. In supplying words to fit the melodies, he performed a feat unique in the history of art. And the fact that he produced some hundreds of songs in his Dumfries days is a noble tribute to his unflagging energy and dedicated labour.

But the flawed heart from the Mount Oliphant days, and the recurring bouts of rheumatic fever, took their toll. He died at the age of thirty-seven in the direst of poverty and haunted by the threat of a debtor's gaol. On the day of his funeral his widow, in childbed, was literally without a shilling.

He was given a grandiose military funeral with an instrumental band playing the 'Dead March in Saul'. As a 'turn out' it was one of the most extraordinary known to history. Had the military not been present, the 'turn out' might have been even more extraordinary.

2

Burns was a genius: a many-sided genius. Despite the fact that he is the most universally-loved poet, he has yet to come into his own. There is no more flaming satire than *Holy Willie's Prayer*. There is no greater tale than *Tam o' Shanter*. If *A Mans a Man for a' that* is the Marseillaise of humanity, *Auld Lang Syne* is the world's 'national' anthem. There is no more tender love song than *O, My Luve's like a red, red, rose*. There is no finer epistle than *The Epistle to Davie*. There is nothing in world literature to equal the shattering, liberating cosmology of *Love and Liberty* . . . The list could be extended. The poet who laughed the Devil out of Hell (and – more difficult – banished him from Scots Presbyterian theology) and they took pity on him; the poet who asserted that the 'light that led astray was light from Heaven', can be measured by no yard-stick known to

9

letters. He is the first poet of common humanity: he is the first poet to transcend poetry.

Just as there can be no greater musician than Beethoven, there can be no greater poet than Burns. Before either can be surpassed, a new race will have to be born – a different and greater species than the *homo sapiens* hitherto known to history.

Should such a 'new species' come to redeem the faults and failings of our common clay, Burns will be honoured as one of the greatest to predict such a possibility. For in a world corrupted, bedevilled and bewildered, Burns firmly believed in the perfectibility of the human race.

This may seem a dubious virtue to readers living at the end of the twentieth century.

For all those who, whatever their faith or lack of faith, respond to the evocations of ordinary mortality, the following pages will give a lifetime of pleasure, inspiration, hope and courage – and the joy of being alive in a world shot through with terror and darkness and fear. It was in such a world that Burns wrote:

'It's coming yet, for a'that, that man to man the world o'er shall brithers be for a' that.' Who are we to say he sang in vain?

Certainly Burns is not for those who mourn, are faint-hearted, lack faith in humanity, or put their trust in legislators; who love without passion and who hate without compassion; who belittle the struggle of man against the Unknown and who blaspheme against the gift of life and put their trust in party politicians. Burns's poems and songs sing of the richness and strangeness and wonder of life. He did not write for those of little faith. Above all, he wrote for those who know that:

'The heart ay's the part ay that makes us right or wrang.'

If Shakespeare (for example) be regarded as the poet who scaled the highest peaks of poetic attainment, few will dispute his unique honour and splendour and glory. But mankind cannot dwell on such peaks of rarefied experience: few indeed ever reach the plodding foothills . . .

But Burns may be likened to the broad rolling plain of mankind's triumph and travail. For here mankind weep and mourn, sing and rejoice, are born and beget their kind and die. In every stage of the journey from the cradle to the grave. Burns is triumphantly articulate.

Chronology of Burns' Life

1759   *January 25.* Robert Burns is born at Alloway, Ayrshire, the eldest son of William Burnes (1721-84) and his wife, Agnes Brown (1732-1820). Their other children were Gilbert (1761-1832), Agnes (1762-1834), Anabella (1764-1832), William (1767-90), John (1769-85) and Isabella (1771-1858). Robert was the first to drop the 'e' from the name.

1765   Robert and Gilbert are sent to school at Alloway Mill. There Burns is influenced by the work of Arthur Masson and a translation of *Wallace* by the 15th-century poet, Blind Harry.

1766   William Burnes rents Mount Oliphant Farm, on part of the Fergusson estate near Alloway.

1772   Robert and Gilbert attend Dalrymple parish school, week about, during the summer quarter.

1775   Burns attends Hugh Rodger's school at Kirkoswald and writes his first love song, 'O, Once I lov'd a bonie lass' for Nelly Kirkpatrick of Dalrymple, with whom he worked on the harvest.

1777   At Whitsun William Burnes moves from

Mount Oliphant to a farm at Lochlie near Tarbolton.

1781   Burns courts Alison Begbie, a servant-girl at a neighbouring farm. She rejects his proposal of marriage but inspires three songs, most notably 'Mary Morison'. In an effort to find a career and to gain financial independence to enable him to marry, Burns and his brother Gilbert go to Irvine about midsummer to train as flax-dressers, work they find monotonous and painful.

1782   *January 1.* The Irvine shop is burnt out and soon after, Burns returns to Lochlie.

1783   *April.* Burns begins his commonplace book, in which he kept notes and wrote poems.

      Autumn. Robert and Gilbert secretly arrange to rent Mossgiel, a farm near Mauchline.

1784   *February 13.* William Burnes dies and the family moves to Mossgiel.

1785   *May 22.* Elizabeth, the poet's daughter by Elizabeth Paton, a girl who had helped out at Lochlie while Burns' father was dying, is born. During the summer Burns meets one of the great loves of his life, Jean Armour.
      September. Burns attests his marriage to Jean Armour.

13

November 1. John Burns, the poet's youngest brother is buried.

During this year Burns began to write his satires, composed 'Love and Liberty', and in October finished his first commonplace book.

1786   *April.* Burns plans to emigrate to Jamaica, after James Armour discovers his daughter is pregnant.

c. April 23. James Armour repudiates Burns as a son-in-law. Burns in turn repudiates Jean Armour.

May 14. Burns' farewell and 'marriage' (the exchange of Bibles) to Mary Campbell, otherwise known as Highland Mary, a nurse-maid Burns had fallen in love with after Jean Armour had been sent to relatives in Paisley by her outraged father.

June 9. Jean returns to Mauchline.

Mid-July. Jean Armour's father attempts to force payment from Burns for her unborn child, in the knowledge that the forthcoming publication of the *Poems* will bring in money.

July 22. Burns transfers his share in Mossgiel to Gilbert, as well as any profits from the *Poems*.

July 30. Burns goes into hiding to avoid James

Armour's writ over his daughter's pregnancy.

July 31. The Kilmarnock Edition *Poems, Chiefly in the Scottish Dialect* is published. Over 600 copies are sold by the end of August.

c. September 1. As his fame spreads, Burns postpones a planned emigration to Jamaica to escape his domestic problems.

September 3. Jean Armour bears Burns twins, who are christened Robert and Jean.

c. September 27. Second postponement of Jamaica voyage.

October. Mary Campbell dies at Greenock of typhus while expecting Burns' child. Burns' finally abandons his Jamaica plans.

November 29. Burns arrives in Edinburgh.

December 9. Henry Mackenzie, a contributor to learned and literary journals, praises the Kilmarnock Edition in the influential Mirror Club's journal, *The Lounger*, of which he was the editor. Burns is proclaimed as the 'ploughman poet'.

1787   *January 13.* The Grand Lodge of Scotland toasts Burns as 'Caledonia's Bard'.

April 21. The Edinburgh Edition of the *Poems* is published.

April 23. Burns sells the copyright in the Edinburgh Edition to William Creech, an Edinburgh publisher, for 100 guineas.

End of May. Volume 1 of the *Scots Musical Museum* is published, to which Burns is a major contributor Burns collected the songs, of which about 160 were his own, for the six volumes published up to 1803.

June 4. Burns receives a letter telling him of the pregnancy of Meg Cameron, an Edinburgh servant-girl.

June 9. Burns returns to Mauchline.

August 8. Burns returns to Edinburgh.

August 15. Burns is freed of Meg Cameron's writ, after he has admitted liability for her pregnancy.

October. The poet's daughter, Jean, dies.

December 6. Burns is introduced to Mrs Agnes Maclehose in the home of a mutual friend. Under the pseudonym of Clarinda, she carried on a well-known correspondence with Burns.

1788   *February 23*. Burns returns to Mauchline from Edinburgh, buys Jean a 'mahogany bed' and sets up house with her, publicly testifying that they are man and wife.

March 3. Jean bears twin girls, of whom one dies on March 10 and the other on March 22.

March 18. Burns signs the lease of Ellisland, a farm near Dumfries.

June 11. Burns settles at Ellisland.

August 5. Rev. William Auld and the Mauchline Kirk Session recognize the authenticity of the marriage of Burns and Jean Armour.

November 5. Jenny Clow, an Edinburgh tavern girl, bears Burns a son.

1789   *February 16*. Burns goes to Edinburgh to close accounts with Creech and (February 27) to settle Jenny Clow's suit.

c. July. Burns meets Francis Grose, an English painter and writer living in Scotland to collect material for his *Antiquities of Scotland*.

August 18. Francis Wallace Burns born.

September. Burns begins work as an Excise officer.

1790   *July*. Burns is transferred to the Dumfries Third Division.

July 24. William Burns, Robert's brother, dies in London.

December 1. Burns sends the manuscript of 'Tam o' Shanter' to Grose.

1791   *March 31*. Anne Park, a barmaid, bears Burns a daughter, Elizabeth. Jean took in the child and raised it as her own.

April 9. William Nicol Burns born.

April. 'Tam o' Shanter', Burns' only narrative poem is published in *Antiquities of Scotland* and in the March issue of the *Edinburgh Magazine*.

September 10. The formal renunciation of Ellisland lease is signed following the farms' failure.

November 11. Burns moves to Dumfries.

December 6. Burns visits Edinburgh to say farewell to Agnes Maclehose, who is due to sail for Jamaica to join her husband. The affair is celebrated in Burns' 'Ae Fond Kiss'.

1792   Burns is promoted to Dumfries Port Division.
April 10. Burns is made an honorary member of the Royal Company of Archers in Edinburgh.

September. Burns begins work for Thomson's *Select Scottish Airs*. He contributed 25 songs to the first volume and a total of 114 to the series of six.

November 21. Elizabeth Riddell Burns is born.

December 31. An Excise inquiry is held into Burns' loyalty, due to his outspoken support for the French Revolution.

1793 *February 18.* The second Edinburgh Edition of *Poems* published.

March. Burns asks for and receives burgess privileges in the Dumfries school. Mrs Maclehose returns from the West Indies as a result of her husband having taken a negro mistress who had borne him several children. Although she wrote to Burns, they never met again.

May 19. Burns moves to a house in Millbrae Vennel, Dumfries.

June. The first volume of Thomson's *Select Scottish Airs* published.

c. August 30. 'Scots Wha Hae', written in honour of Robert the Bruce's victory at Bannockburn in 1314, is sent to Thomson. Due to a disagreement over words and tune, it wasn't published in Burns' lifetime. It has since been adopted as a national song.

c. December 31. Beginning of the Riddell quarrel. Burns had had a close relationship with Maria Banks Riddell but this was brought to a temporary end when he was banished from her sister-in-law's house after a drunken revel.

1794   *c. May 1*. Burns declines a post on the *Morning Chronicle*, London.

August 12. James Glencairn Burns is born.

c. December 22. Burns is appointed Acting Supervisor at Dumfries for four months until the recovery from illness of the holder of the post.

1795   *September*. Death of Elizabeth Riddell Burns, Burns' daughter, at Mossgiel.

1796   *July 21*. Robert Burns dies of endocarditis induced by rheumatism.

July 25. Burns is buried in Dumfries, the same day his son Maxwell is born.

c.1801   The first Burns Club is established in the poet's honour in Greenock.

1815   First Burns Supper to be held in Edinburgh.

Love and Liberty

A Cantata

RECITATIVO

1

withered; ground	When lyart leaves bestrow the yird,
	Or, wavering like the bauckie-bird,
	Bedim cauld Boreas' blast;
lash	When hailstanes drive wi' bitter skyte,
	And infant frosts begin to bite,
rime	In hoary cranreuch drest;
One; gang	Ae night at e'en a merry core
lawless; vagrant carousal	O' randie, gangrel bodies
	In Poosie-Nansie's held the splore,
spare rags	To drink their orra duddies:
	Wi' quaffing and laughing
roistered	They ranted an' they sang,
	Wi' jumping an' thumping
very	The vera girdle rang.

4

next	First, niest the fire, in auld red rags
	Ane sat, weel brac'd wi' mealy bags
	And knapsack a' in order;
	His doxy lay within his arm;
whisky	Wi' usquebae an' blankets warm,
leered	She blinket on her sodger.
flushed with drink	An' ay he gies the tozie drab
sounding	The tither skelpin kiss,

While she held up her greedy gab   mouth
  Just like an aumous dish: alms-dish
    Ilk smack still did crack still   Each
      Like onie cadger's whup;   hawker's
    Then, swaggering an' staggering,
      He roar'd this ditty up:–

SONG

TUNE: Soldiers Joy

1

I am a son of Mars, who have been in many wars,
  And show my cuts and scars wherever I come:
This here was for a wench, and that other in a trench,
  When welcoming the French at the sound of the drum.
                Lal de daudle, *etc.*

2

My prenticeship I past, where my leader breath'd his last,
  When the bloody die was cast on the heights of Abram;
And I servèd out my trade when the gallant game
    was play'd,
  And the Moro low was laid at the sound of the drum.

3

I lastly was with Curtis among the floating batt'ries,
  And there I left for witness an arm and a limb;
Yet let my country need me, with Eliott to head me
  I'd clatter on my stumps at the sound of the drum.

4

And now, tho' I must beg with a wooden arm and leg,

And many a tatter'd rag hanging over my bum,
I'm as happy with my wallet, my bottle, and my callet
    As when I us'd in scarlet to follow a drum.

5

What tho' with hoary locks I must stand the winter
        shocks,
    Beneath the woods and rocks oftentimes for a
        home?

trull When the tother bag I sell, and the tother bottle tell,
    I could meet a troop of Hell at the sound of a drum.

RECITATIVO

rafters shook He ended; and the kebars sheuk
Over   Aboon the chorus roar;
rats While frighted rattons backward leuk,
inmost hole   An' seek the benmost bore:
tiny; corner A fairy fiddler frae the neuk,
squeaked   He skirl'd out *Encore!*
dear But up arose the martial chuck,
        An' laid the loud uproar:–

SONG
TUNE: Sodger Laddie

1

I once was a maid, tho' I cannot tell when
And still my delight is in proper young men.
Some one of a troop of dragoons was my daddie:
No wonder I'm fond of a sodger laddie!
            Sing, lal de dal, *etc.*

23

2

The first of my loves was a swaggering blade:
To rattle the thundering drum was his trade;
His leg was so tight, and his cheek was so ruddy,
Transported I was with my sodger laddie.

3

But the godly old chaplain left him in the lurch;
The sword I forsook for the sake of the church;
He riskèd the soul, and I ventur'd the body:
'Twas then I prov'd false to my sodger laddie.

4

Full soon I grew sick of my sanctified sot;
The regiment at large for a husband I got;
From the gilded spontoon to the fife I was ready
I askèd no more but a sodger laddie,

5

But the Peace it reduc'd me to beg in despair,
Till I met my old boy in a Cunningham Fair;
His rags regimental they flutter'd so gaudy:
My heart it rejoic'd at a sodger laddie.

6

And now I have liv'd – I know not how long!
But still I can join in a cup and a song;
And whilst with both hands I can hold the glass
steady,
Here's to thee, my hero, my sodger laddie!

RECITATIVO

Poor Merry-Andrew in the neuk
Sat guzzling wi' a tinkler-hizzie;
They mind't na wha the chorus teuk,
    Between themselves they were sae busy.
    At length, wi' drink an' courting dizzy,
He stoiter'd up an' made a face;
    Then turn'd an' laid a smack on Grizzie,
Syne tun'd his pipes wi' grave grimace:–

tinker-wench
cared not; took

struggled

Then

SONG

TUNE: Auld Sir Symon

1

Sir Wisdom's a fool when he's fou;
    Sir Knave is a fool in a session:
He's there but a prentice I trow,
    But I am a fool by profession.

drunk
court

2

My grannie she bought me a beuk,
    An' I held awa to the school:
I fear I my talent misteuk,
    But what will ye hae of a fool?

book
went off

3

For drink I wad venture my neck;
    A hizzie's the half of my craft:
But what could ye other expect
    Of ane that's avowedly daft?

cracked

4

I ance was tyed up like a stirk   *bullock*
  For civilly swearing and quaffing;
I ance was abus'd i' the kirk   *rebuked*
  For towsing a lass i' my daffin.   *rumpling; fun*

5

Poor Andrew that tumbles for sport
  Let naebody name wi' a jeer:
There's even, I'm tauld, i' the Court
  A tumbler ca'd the Premier.

6

Observ'd ye yon reverend lad
  Mak faces to tickle the mob?
He rails at our mountebank squad –
  It's rivalship just i' the job!

7

And now my conclusion I'll tell,
  For faith! I'm confoundedly dry:
The chiel that's a fool for himsel,   *fellow*
  Guid Lord! he's far dafter than I.

RECITATIVO

Then niest outspak a raucle carlin,   *sturdy hag*
Wha kent fu' weel to cleek the sterlin,
For monie a purse she had hookèd,   *ducked*
An' had in monie a well been doukèd.
Her love had been a Highland laddie,
But weary fa' the waefu' woodie!   *plague upon;*
                                       gallows

Wi' sighs an' sobs she thus began
To wail her braw John Highlandman:–

fine

SONG

TUNE: O' An Ye Were Dead, Guidman

Chorus

Sing hey my braw John Highlandman!
Sing ho my braw John Highlandman!
There's not a lad in a' the lan'
Was match for my John Highlandman!

1

A Highland lad my love was born,
The lalland laws he held in scorn,
But he still was faithfu' to his clan,
My gallant, braw John Highlandman.

lowland

2

With his philibeg, an' tartan plaid,
An' guid claymore down by his side,
The ladies' hearts he did trepan,
My gallant, braw John Highlandman.

kilt

3

We rangèd a' from Tweed to Spey,
An' liv'd like lords an' ladies gay,
For a lalland face he fearèd none,
My gallant, braw John Highlandman.

4

They banish'd him beyond the sea,

But ere the bud was on the tree,
Adown my cheeks the pearls ran,
Embracing my John Highlandman.

5

But Och! they catch'd him at the last,
And bound him in a dungeon fast.
My curse upon them every one –
They've hang'd my braw John Highlandman!

6

And now a widow I must mourn
The pleasures that will ne'er return;
No comfort but a hearty can
When I think on John Highlandman.

RECITATIVO

1

A pigmy scraper on a fiddle,
Wha us'd to trystes an' fairs to driddle,
Her strappin limb an' gawsie middle   buxom
    (He reach'd nae higher)
Had hol'd his heartie like a riddle,
    An' blawn't on fire.   blown it

2

Wi' hand on hainch and upward e'e,   hip
He croon'd his gamut, one, two, three,   hummed
Then in an *arioso* key
    The wee Apollo
Set off wi' *allegretto* glee
    His *giga* solo:–

SONG

rest

TUNE: *Whistle Owre the Lave O't*

Chorus
I am a fiddler to my trade,
An' a' the tunes that e'er I play'a,
The sweetest still to wife or maid
    Was Whistle Owre the Lave O't.

1

reach; wipe

Let me ryke up to dight that tear;
An' go wi' me an' be my dear,
An' then your every care an' fear
    May whistle owre the lave o't.

2

harvest-homes;
we'll

At kirns an' weddins we'se be there,
An' O, sae nicely 's we will fare!
We'll bowse about till Daddie Care
    Sing *Whistle Owre the Lave O't.*

3

bones; pick

fence

Sae merrily the banes we'll pyke,
An' sun ousels about the dyke;
An' at our leisure, when ye like,
    We'll – whistle owre the lave o't!

4

tickle; catgut

such

But bless me wi' your heav'n o' charms,
An' while I kittle hair on thairms,
Hunger, cauld, an' a' sic harms
    May whistle owre the lave o't.

RECITATIVO

1

Her charms had struck a sturdy caird | tinker
  As weel as poor gut-scraper;
He taks the fiddler by the beard,
  An' draws a roosty rapier; | rusty
He swoor by a' was swearing worth
  To speet him like a pliver, | plover
Unless he would from that time forth
  Relinquish her for ever.

2

Wi' ghastly e'e poor Tweedle-Dee
  Upon his hunkers bended, | hams
An' pray'd for grace wi' ruefu' face,
  An' sae the quarrel ended. | so
But tho' his little heart did grieve
  When round the tinkler prest her,
He feign'd to snirtle in his sleeve | snigger
  When thus the caird address'd her:–

SONG

TUNE: Clout the Cauldron | Patch

1

My bonie lass, I work in brass,
  A tinkler is my station;
I've travell'd round all Christian ground
  In this my occupation;
I've taen the gold, an' been enrolled

In many a noble squadron;
But vain they search'd when off I march'd
    To go an' clout the cauldron.

2

Despise that shrimp, that wither'd imp,
    With a' his noise an' cap'rin,
An' take a share wi' those that bear
    The budget and the apron!
pot   And by that stowp, my faith an' houpe!
    And by that dear Kilbaigie!
short commons   If e'er ye want, or meet wi' scant,
wet; throat   May I ne'er weet my craigie!

RECITATIVO

1

The caird prevail'd: th' unblushing fair
    In his embraces sunk,
Partly wi' love o'ercome sae sair,
    An' partly she was drunk.
Sir Violino, with an air
spirit   That show'd a man o' spunk.
Wish'd unison between the pair,
    An' made the bottle clunk
            To their health that night.

2

urchin   But hurchin Cupid shot a shaft,
trick   That play'd a dame a shavie:
The fiddler rak'd her fore and aft
hencoop   Behint the chicken cavie;

Her lord, a wight of Homer's craft,
  Tho' limpin' wi' the spavie,
He hirpl'd up, an lap like daft,
  An' shor'd them 'Dainty Davie'
        O' boot that night.

*spavin
hobbled; leapt
like mad
offered*

Gratis

3

He was a care-defying blade
  As ever Bacchus listed!
Tho' Fortune sair upon him laid,
  His heart, she ever miss'd it.
He had no wish but – to be glad,
  Nor want but – when he thristed,
He hated nought but – to be sad;
  An' thus the Muse suggested
        His sang that night:–

SONG

TUNE: For A' That, An' A' That

Chorus

*For a' that, an' a' that,
An' twice as muckle's a' that,
I've lost but ane, I've twa behin',
I've wife eneugh for a' that.*

much

1

I am a Bard, of no regard
  Wi' gentle folks an' a' that,
But Homer-like the glowrin byke,
  Frae town to town I draw that.

staring crowd

2

pond   I never drank the Muses' stank,
brook   Castalia's burn, an' a' that;
foams   But there it streams, an' richly reams –
       My Helicon I ca' that.

3

Great love I bear to a' the fair,
   Their humble slave an' a' that;
But lordly will, I hold it still
thwart   A mortal sin to thraw that.

4

In raptures sweet this hour we meet
   Wi' mutual love an' a' that;
fly; sting   But for how lang the flie may stang,
    Let inclination law that!

5

Their tricks an' craft hae put me daft,
   They've taen me in, an' a' that;
But clear your decks, an' here's the Sex!
   I like the jads for a' that.

Chorus

For a' that, an' a' that,
much   *An' twice as muckle's a' that,*
My dearest bluid, to do them guid,
to it   *They're welcome till't for a' that!*

RECITATIVO

So sung the Bard, and Nansie's wa's   walls
Shook with a thunder of applause,
  Re-echo'd from each mouth!
They toom'd their pocks, they pawn'd their duds, emptied their
               bags
They scarcely left to coor their fuds,   cover; tails
  To quench their lowin drouth.   burning
Then owre again the jovial thrang   company
  The Poet did request
To lowse his pack, an' wale a sang,   untie; choose
   A ballad o' the best:
    He rising, rejoicing
     Between his twa Deborahs,
    Looks round him, an' found them
     Impatient for the chorus:–

SONG

TUNE: *Jolly Mortals, Fill Your Glasses*

Chorus

A fig for those by law protected!
 Liberty's a glorious feast,
Courts for cowards were erected,
 Churches built to please the priest!

1

See the smoking bowl before us!
 Mark our jovial, ragged ring!
Round and round take up the chorus,
 And in raptures let us sing:

2

What is title, what is treasure,
  What is reputation's care?
If we lead a life of pleasure,
  'Tis no matter how or where!

3

With the ready trick and fable
  Round we wander all the day;
And at night in barn or stable
  Hug our doxies on the hay.

4

Does the train-attended carriage
  Thro' the country lighter rove?
Does the sober bed of marriage
  Witness brighter scenes of love?

5

Life is all a variorum,
  We regard not how it goes;
Let them prate about decorum,
  Who have character to lose.

6

Here's to budgets, bags and wallets!
  Here's to all the wandering train!
Here's our ragged brats and callets!
  One and all, cry out, Amen!

The Twa Dogs

A Tale

'Twas in that place o' Scotland's isle
That bears the name of auld King Coil,
Upon a bonie day in June,
When wearing thro' the afternoon,
Twa dogs, that were na thrang at hame,   *busy*
Forgathered ance upon a time.   *chance-met*

 The first I'll name, they ca'd him Cæsar,
Was keepit for 'his Honor's' pleasure:
His hair, his size, his mouth, his lugs,   *ears*
Shew'd he was nane o' Scotland's dogs;
But whalpit some place far abroad,
Where sailors gang to fish for cod.

 His lockèd, letter'd, braw brass collar
Shew'd him the gentleman an' scholar;
But tho' he was o' high degree,
The fient a pride, nae pride had he;   *fiend*
But wad hae spent an hour caressin,
Ev'n wi' a tinkler-gipsy's messin;   *mongrel*
At kirk or market, mill or smiddie,   *smithy*
Nae tawted tyke, tho' e'er sae duddie,   *matted cur; ragged*
But he wad stan't, as glad to see him,   *would have stood*
An' stroan't on stanes an' hillocks wi' him.   *urinated*

 The tither was a ploughman's collie,
A rhyming, ranting, raving billie,   *rollicking; blade*

Wha for his friend an' comrade had him,
And in his freaks had Luath ca'd him,
After some dog in Highland sang,
Was made lang syne – Lord knows how lang.

He was a gash an' faithfu' tyke,
As ever lap a sheugh or dyke.
His honest, sonsie, baws'nt face
Ay gat him friend in ilka place;
His breast was white, his tousie back
Weel clad wi' coat o' glossy black;
His gawsie tail, wi' upward curl,
Hung owre his hurdies wi' a swirl.

Nae doubt but they were fain o' ither,
And unco pack an' thick thegither;
Wi' social nose whyles snuff'd an' snowkit;
Whyles mice an' moudieworts they howkit;
Whyles scour'd awa' in lang excursion,
An' worry'd ither in diversion;
Till tir'd at last wi' monie a farce,
They sat them down upon their arse,
An' there began a lang digression
About the 'lords o' the creation.'

CÆSAR

I've aften wonder'd, honest Luath,
What sort o' life poor dogs like you have;
An' when the gentry's life I saw,
What way poor bodies liv'd ava.

Marginal glosses:
wise
ditch; stone fence
pleasant, white-streaked
every
shaggy

joyous
buttocks

glad in
confidential
now
moles; dug

at all

Our laird gets in his rackèd rents,   *rents in kind;*
His coals, his kain, an' a' his stents: *dues*
He rises when he likes himsel;
His flunkies answer at the bell;
He ca's his coach; he ca's his horse;
He draws a bonie silken purse,
As lang's my tail, whare, thro' the steeks,   *stitches*
The yellow letter'd Geordie keeks.   *guinea peeps*

Frae morn to e'en it's nought but toiling,
At baking, roasting, frying, boiling;
An' tho' the gentry first are stechin,   *cramming*
Yet ev'n the ha' folk fill their pechan *servants; stomach*
Wi' sauce, ragouts, an sic like trashtrie,
That's little short o' downright wastrie:
Our whipper-in, wee, blastit wonner,
Poor, worthless elf, it eats a dinner,
Better than onie tenant-man
His Honour has in a' the lan';
An' what poor cot-folk pit their painch in, *put; paunch*
I own it's past my comprehension.

LUATH

Trowth, Cæsar, whyles they're fash't eneugh: *sometimes; bothered*
A cotter howkin in a sheugh,   *digging*
Wi' dirty stanes biggin a dyke,   *building*
Baring a quarry, an' sic like;   *clearing*
Himsel, a wife, he thus sustains,
A smytrie o' wee duddie weans,   *litter; brats*
An' nought but his han' darg to keep *hands' labour*
Them right an' tight in thack an' rape. *thatch and rope*

An' when they meet wi' sair disasters,
Like loss o' health or want o' masters,
Ye maist wad think, a wee touch langer,
An' they maun starve o' cauld and hunger:
But how it comes, I never kend yet,
They're maistly wonderfu' contented;
An' buirdly chiels, an' clever hizzies,
Are bred in sic a way as this is.

small

*stout lads;
young women*

CÆSAR

But then to see how ye're negleckit,
How huff'd, an' cuff'd, an' disrespeckit!
Lord man, our gentry care as little
For delvers, ditchers, an' sic cattle;
They gang as saucy by poor folk,
As I wad by a stinking brock.

badger

I've notic'd, on our laird's court-day,
(An' monie a time my heart's been wae),
Poor tenant bodies, scant o' cash,
How they maun thole a factor's snash:
He'll stamp an threaten, curse an' swear
He'll apprehend them, poind their gear;
While they maun staun', wi' aspect humble,
An' hear it a', an' fear an' tremble!
I see how folk live that hae riches;
But surely poor-folk maun be wretches!

sad

*endure;
abuse*

seize

stand

LUATH

They're nae sae wretched 's ane wad think:

Tho' constantly on poortith's brink,   *poverty's*
They're sae accustom'd wi' the sight,
The view o't gies them little fright.

    Then chance an' fortune are sae guided,
They're ay in less or mair provided;
An' tho' fatigu'd wi' close employment,
A blink o' rest's a sweet enjoyment.   *snatch*

    The dearest comfort o' their lives,
Their grushie weans an' faithfu' wives;   *growing*
The prattling things are just their pride,
That sweetens a' their fire-side.

    An' whyles twalpennie worth o' nappy   *sometimes*
Can make the bodies unco happy:
They lay aside their private cares,
To mind the Kirk and State affairs;
They'll talk o' patronage an' priests,
Wi' kindling fury i' their breasts,
Or tell what new taxation's comin,
An' ferlie at the folk in Lon'on.   *marvel*

    As bleak-fac'd Hallowmass returns,   *harvest-homes*
They get the jovial, ranting kirns,
When rural life, of ev'ry station,
Unite in common recreation;
Love blinks, Wit slaps, an' social Mirth   *glances*
Forgets there's Care upo' the earth.

    That merry day the year begins,
They bar the door on frosty win's;
The nappy reeks wi' mantling ream,   *cream*

An' sheds a heart-inspiring steam;
smoking; snuff-box   The luntin pipe, an' sneeshin mill,
Are handed round wi' right guid will;
chatting   The cantie auld folks crackin crouse,
romping   The young anes ranting thro' the house –
My heart has been sae fain to see them,
That I for joy hae barkit wi' them.

Still it's owre true that ye hae said
too often   Sic game is now owre aften play'd;
There's monie a creditable stock
well-doing   O' decent, honest, fawsont folk,
Are riven out baith root an' branch,
Some rascal's pridefu' greed to quench,
Wha thinks to knit himself the faster
In favor wi' some gentle master,
may be   Wha, aiblins thrang a parliamentin',
indenturing   For Britain's guid his saul indentin'–

CÆSAR

Haith, lad, ye little ken about it:
For Britain's guid! guid faith! I doubt it.
Say rather, gaun as Premiers lead him:
An' saying aye or no 's they bid him:
At operas an' plays parading,
Mortgaging, gambling, masquerading:
Or maybe, in a frolic daft,
To Hague or Calais taks a waft,
To mak a tour an' tak a whirl,
To learn *bon ton,* an' see the worl'.

There, at Vienna or Versailles,
He rives his father's auld entails;   splits
Or by Madrid he taks the rout,   road
To thrum guitars an' fecht wi' nowt;   fight; cattle
Or down Italian vista startles,   courses
Whore-hunting amang groves o' myrtles
Then bowses drumlie German-water,   muddy
To mak himsel look fair an' fatter,
An' purge the bitter ga's an' cankers   venereal sores
O' curst Venetian bores an' chancres.

For Britain's guid! for her destruction!
Wi' dissipation, feud an' faction.

LUATH

Hech man! dear sirs! is that the gate   way
They waste sae monie a braw estate!
Are we sae foughten an' harass'd   troubled
For gear ta gang that gate at last?   wealth to go

O would they stay aback frae courts,
An' please themsels wi' countra sports,
It wad for ev'ry ane be better,
The laird, the tenant, an' the cotter!
For thae frank, rantin, ramblin billies,   those; roistering
Fient haet o' them's ill-hearted fellows: Not one
Except for breakin o' their timmer,   wasting their woods
Or speakin lightly o' their limmer,   mistress
Or shootin of a hare or moor-cock,
The ne'er-a-bit they're ill to poor folk.

But will ye tell me, master Cæsar:
Sure great folk's life's a life o' pleasure?
touch Nae cauld nor hunger e'er can steer them,
The vera thought o't need na fear them.

CÆSAR

Lord, man, were ye but whyles whare I am,
The gentles, ye wad ne'er envy 'em!

It's true, they need na starve or sweat,
Thro' winter's cauld, or simmer's heat;
hard They've nae sair wark to craze their banes,
gripes and An' fill auld-age wi' grips an' granes:
groans But human bodies are sic fools,
For a' their colleges an' schools,
That when nae real ills perplex them,
fret They mak enow themsels to vex them;
An' ay the less they hae to sturt them,
In like proportion, less will hurt them.

A countra fellow at the pleugh,
His acre's till'd, he's right eneugh;
A countra girl at her wheel,
dozen Her dizzen's done, she's unco weel;
But gentlemen, an' ladies warst,
positive Wi' ev'n down want o' wark are curst:
They loiter, lounging, lank an' lazy;
nothing Tho' deil-haet ails them, yet uneasy:
Their days insipid, dull an' tasteless;
Their nights unquiet, lang an' restless.

An' ev'n their sports, their balls an' races,
Their galloping through public places,
There's sic parade, sic pomp an' art,
The joy can scarcely reach the heart.

The men cast out in party-matches,   *solder*
Then sowther a' in deep debauches;   *One*
Ae night they're mad wi' drink an' whoring,   *Next*
Niest day their life is past enduring.

The ladies arm-in-arm in clusters,
As great an' gracious a' as sisters;
But hear their absent thoughts o' ither,   *downright*
They're a' run deils an' jads thegither.
Whyles, owre the wee bit cup an' platie,
They sip the scandal-potion pretty;   *live-long*
Or lee-lang nights, wi' crabbit leuks   *books*
Pore owre the devil's pictur'd beuks;
Stake on a chance a farmer's stackyard,
An' cheat like onie unhang'd blackguard.

There's some exceptions, man an' woman;
But this is Gentry's life in common.

By this, the sun was out o' sight,
An' darker gloamin brought the night;   *twilight*
The bum-clock humm'd wi' lazy drone;   *beetle*
The kye stood rowtin' i' the loan;   *cattle; lowing;*
                                             grassy track
When up they gat, an' shook their lugs,
Rejoic'd they were na *men*, but *dogs*;
An' each took aff his several way,
Resolv'd to meet some ither day.

The Author's Earnest Cry and Prayer

TO THE SCOTCH REPRESENTATIVES IN THE HOUSE OF COMMONS

Dearest of distillation! last and best –
– How art thou lost! –

PARODY ON MILTON

1

Ye Irish lords, ye knights an' squires,
Wha represent our brughs an' shires,
prudently   An' doucely manage our affairs
           In Parliament,
To you a simple Bardie's prayers
           Are humbly sent.

2

hoarse   Alas! my roupet Muse is haerse!
Your Honors' hearts wi' grief 'twad pierce,
To see her sittin on her arse
           Low i' the dust,
And scriechin out prosaic verse,
           An' like to brust!

3

Tell them wha hae the chief direction,
Scotland an' me's in great affliction,
E'er sin' they laid that curst restriction
           On aqua-vitae;
An' rouse them up to strong conviction,
           An' move their pity.

4

Stand forth, an' tell yon Premier youth
The honest, open, naked truth:
Tell him o' mine an' Scotland's drouth,   *thirst*
         His servants humble:
The muckle deevil blaw you south,
         If ye dissemble!

5

Does onie great man glunch an' gloom?   *growl*
Speak out, an' never fash your thumb!   *care a rap*
Let posts an' pensions sink or soom   *swim*
         Wi' them wha grant 'em:
If honestly they canna come,
         Far better want 'em.

6

In gath'rin votes you were na slack;
Now stand as tightly by your tack:
Ne'er claw your lug, an' fidge your back,   *scratch; wriggle*
         An' hum an haw;
But raise your arm, an' tell your crack   *tale*
         Before them a'.

7

Paint Scotland greetin owre her thrissle;   *weeping; thistle*
Her mutchkin stowp as toom's a whissle;   *pint-pot; empty*
An' damn'd excisemen in a bustle,
         Seizin a stell,   *still*
Triumphant, crushin't like a mussel,
         Or lampit shell!   *limpet*

8

Then, on the tither hand, present her –
A blackguard smuggler right behint her,
An' cheek-for-chow, a chuffie vintner
        Colleaguing join,
Pickin her pouch as bare as winter
        Of a' kind coin.

cheek-by-jowl;
fat-faced

pocket

9

Is there, that bears the name o' Scot,
But feels his heart's bluid rising hot,
To see his poor auld mither's pot
        Thus dung in staves,
An' plunder'd o' her hindmost groat,
        By gallows knaves?

broken in
pieces

10

Alas! I'm but a nameless wight,
Trode i' the mire out o' sight!
But could I like Montgomeries fight,
        Or gab like Boswell,
There's some sark-necks I wad draw tight,
        An' tie some hose well.

speak

shirt-

11

God bless your Honors! can ye see't,
The kind, auld, cantie carlin greet,
An' no get warmly to your feet,
        An' gar them hear it,
An' tell them wi' a patriot-heat,
        Ye winna bear it?

jolly matron
weep

make

12

Some o' you nicely ken the laws,
To round the period an' pause,
An' with rhetòric clause on clause
   To mak harangues:
Then echo thro' Saint Stephen's wa's
   Auld Scotland's wrangs.

13

Dempster, a true blue Scot I'se warran;
Thee, aith-detesting, chaste Kilkerran;   oath-
An' that glib-gabbet Highland baron, smooth-tongued
   The Laird o' Graham;
An' ane, a chap that's damn'd auldfarran, shrewd
   Dundas his name:

14

Erskine, a spunkie Norland billie; sprightful fellow
True Campbells, Frederick and Ilay;
An' Livistone, the bauld Sir Willie;
   An' monie ithers
Whom auld Demosthenes or Tully
   Might own for brithers.

15

Thee sodger Hugh, my watchman stented, assigned
If Bardies e'er are represented;
I ken if that your sword were wanted,
   Ye'd lend your hand
But when there's ought to say anent it,
   Ye're at a stand.

16

Arouse' my boys! exert your mettle,
To get auld Scotland back her kettle;
Or faith! I'll wad my new pleugh-pettle,
        Ye'll see 't or lang,
She'll teach you, wi' a reekin whittle,
        Anither sang.

bet:
plough-staff

smoking knife

17

This while she's been in crankous mood,
Her lost Militia fir'd her bluid;
(Deil na they never mair do guid,
        Play'd her that pliskie!)
An' now she's like to rin red-wud
        About her whisky.

fretful

trick

stark-mad

18

An' Lord! if ance they pit her till't
Her tartan petticoat she'll kilt,
An durk an' pistol at her belt,
        She'll tak the streets,
An' rin her whittle to the hilt,
        I' the first she meet!

put her to 't
tuck up

knife

19

For God-sake, sirs! then speak her fair,
An' straik her cannie wi' the hair,
An' to the Muckle House repair,
        Wi' instant speed,
An' strive, wi' a' your wit an' lear,
        To get remead.

stroke; gently
the Commons

learning
redress

20

Yon ill-tongu'd tinkler, Charlie Fox,
May taunt you wi' his jeers an' mocks;
But gie him't het, my hearty cocks!   *hot*
      E'en cowe the cadie!   *scare the varlet*
An' send him to his dicing box
      An' sportin lady.

21

Tell yon guid bluid of auld Boconnock's,
I'll be his debt twa mashlum bonnocks,   *mixed-meal*
An' drink his health in auld Nanse Tinnock's   *bannocks*
      Nine times a-week.
If he some scheme, like tea an' winnocks,   *windows*
      Wad kindly seek.

22

Could he some commutation broach,
I'll pledge my aith in guid braid Scotch,
He needna fear their foul reproach
      Nor erudition,
Yon mixtie-maxtie, queer hotch-potch,   *mixed-up*
      The Coalition.

23

Auld Scotland has a raucle tongue;   *bitter*
She's just a devil wi' a rung;   *cudgel*
An' if she promise auld or young
      To tak their part,
Tho' by the neck she should be strung,
      She'll no desert.

24

And now, ye chosen Five-and-Forty,
May still your mither's heart support ye;
pettish   Then, tho' a minister grow dorty,
         An' kick your place,
Ye'll snap your fingers, poor an' hearty,
            Before his face.

25

God bless your Honors, a' your days,
sups; broth;   Wi' sowps o' kail and brats o' claes,
scraps; clothes
jack-daws   In spite o' a' the thievish kaes,
          That haunt St. Jamie's!
Your humble Bardie sings an' prays,
          While Rab his name is.

POSTCRIPT

26

Let half-starv'd slaves in warmer skies
See future wines, rich-clust'ring, rise;
Their lot auld Scotland ne'er envies,
          But, blythe and frisky,
She eyes her freeborn, martial boys
          Tak aff their whisky.

27

sun   What tho' their Phoebus kinder warms,
While fragrance blooms and Beauty charms,
When wretches range, in famish'd swarms,
          The scented groves;

Or, hounded forth, dishonor arms
        In hungry droves!

28

Their gun's a burden on their shouther;
They downa bide the stink o' powther;   *cannot*
Their bauldest thought's a hank'ring swither   *doubt*
        To stan' or rin,
Till skelp – a shot – they're aff, a' throw'ther,   *°crack; pell-mell*
        To save their skin.

29

But bring a Scotsman frae his hill,
Clap in his cheek a Highland gill,   *Put in his mouth*
Say, such is royal George's will,
        An' there's the foe!
He has nae thought but how to kill
        Twa at a blow.

30

Nae cauld, faint-hearted doubtings tease him;
Death comes, wi' fearless eye he sees him;
Wi' bluidy han' a welcome gies him;
        An' when he fa's,
His latest draught o' breathin lea'es him
        In faint huzzas.

31

eyes; shut
smoke

Sages their solemn een may steek
An' raise a philosophic reek,
An' physically causes seek
        In clime an' season;
But tell me whisky's name in Greek:
        I'll tell the reason.

32

sometimes
heather-tops
lose; water

Scotland, my auld, respected mither!
Tho' whiles ye moistify your leather,
Till whare ye sit on craps o' heather
        Ye tine your dam,
Freedom and whisky gang thegither,
        Tak aff your dram!

The Holy Fair

A robe of seeming truth and trust
  Hid crafty observation;
And secret hung, with poison'd crust,
  The dirk of defamation:
A mask that like the gorget show'd,
  Dye-varying on the pigeon;
And for a mantle large and broad,
  He wrapt him in Religion.
                HYPOCRISY À-LA-MODE

1

Upon a simmer Sunday morn,
  When Nature's face is fair,
I walkèd forth to view the corn,
  An' snuff the caller air.   cool
The rising sun, owre Galston Muirs,
  Wi' glorious light was glintin;   glancing
    The hares were hirplin down the furs,   hopping; furrows
The lav'rocks they were chantin   larks
            Fu' sweet that day.

2

As lightsomely I glowr'd abroad,   gazed
  To see a scene sae gay,
Three hizzies, early at the road,   young women
  Cam skelpin up the way.   spanking
Twa had manteeles o' dolefu' black,
  But ane wi' lyart lining;   grey
The third, that gaed a wee a-back,   walked a bit
  Was in the fashion shining   behind
            Fu' gay that day.

3

The twa appear'd like sisters twin,
　　In feature, form, an' claes;
Their visage wither'd, lang an' thin,
　　An' sour as onie slaes:
The third cam up, hap-step-an'-lowp,
　　As light as onie lambie,
An' wi' a curchie low did stoop,
　　As soon as e'er she saw me,
　　　　　Fu' kind that day.

4

Wi' bonnet aff, quoth I, 'Sweet lass,
　　I think ye seem to ken me;
I'm sure I've seen that bonie face,
　　But yet I canna name ye.'
Quo' she, an' laughin as she spak,
　　An' taks me by the han's,
'Ye, for my sake, hae gi'en the feck
　　Of a' the Ten Comman's
　　　　　A screed some day.

5

'My name is Fun – your cronie dear,
　　The nearest friend ye hae;
An' this is Superstition here,
　　An' that's Hypocrisy.
I'm gaun to Mauchline Holy Fair,
　　To spend an hour in daffin:
Gin ye'll go there, yon runkl'd pair,
　　We will get famous laughin
　　　　　At them this day.'

Marginal glosses:
- clothes
- hop; jump
- curtsey
- bulk
- rip
- going
- larking
- wrinkled

6

Quoth I, 'Wi' a' my heart, I'll do't;
    I'll get my Sunday's sark on,   *shirt*
An' meet you on the holy spot;
    Faith, we'se hae fine remarkin'!   *we'll*
Then I gaed hame at crowdie-time,   *went; porridge*
    An' soon I made me ready;
For roads were clad, frae side to side,
    Wi' monie a wearie body,
           In droves that day.

7

Here farmers gash, in ridin graith,   *self-complacent; gear*
    Gaed hoddin by their cotters;   *jogging*
There swankies young, in braw braid-claith, . *strapping*
    Are springin owre the gutters.   *lads*
The lasses, skelpin barefit, thrang,   *padding;*
    In silks an' scarlets glitter;   *thronging*
Wi' sweet-milk cheese, in monie a whang,   *shive*
    An' farls, bak'd wi' butter,   *small cakes*
           Fu' crump that day.   *crisp*

8

When by the plate we set our nose,
    Weel heapèd up wi' ha'pence,
A greedy glowr black-bonnet throws,   *the Elder*
    An' we maun draw our tippence.
Then in we go to see the show:
    On ev'ry side they're gath'rin;
Some carryin dails, some chairs an' stools,   *planks*
    An' some are busy bleth'rin   *gabbling*
           Right loud that day.

9

keep off	Here stands a shed to fend the show'rs,
	An' screen our countra gentry;
two or three	There Racer Jess, an' twa-three whores,
leering	Are blinkin at the entry.
whispering jades	Here sits a raw o' tittlin jads,
	Wi' heavin breasts an' bare neck;
weaver	An' there a batch o' wabster lads,
	Blackguardin frae Kilmarnock,
	For fun this day.

10

	Here some are thinkin on their sins,
	An' some upo' their claes;
soiled	Ane curses feet that fyl'd his shins,
	Anither sighs an' prays:
sample	On this hand sits a chosen swatch,
	Wi' screw'd-up, grace-proud faces;
	On that a set o' chaps, at watch,
Busy	Thrang winkin on the lasses
	To chairs that day.

11

	O happy is that man an' blest!
	Nae wonder that it pride him!
	Whase ain dear lass, that he likes best,
	Comes clinkin down beside him!
	Wi' arm repos'd on the chair back,
	He sweetly does compose him;
	Which, by degrees, slip round her neck,
And his palm	An's loof upon her bosom,
	Unkend that day.

57

12

Now a' the congregation o'er
  Is silent expectation;
For Moodie speels the holy door,   *climbs*
  Wi' tidings o' damnation:
Should Hornie, as in ancient days,
  'Mang sons o' God present him;
The vera sight o' Moodie's face   *the Devil*
  To 's ain het hame had sent him;   *hot*
         Wi' fright that day.

13

Hear how he clears the points o' Faith
  Wi' rattlin and thumpin!
Now meekly calm, now wild in wrath,
  He's stampin, an' he's jumpin!
His lengthen'd chin, his turn'd-up snout,
  His eldritch squeel an' gestures,   *unearthly*
O how they fire the heart devout –
  Like cantharidian plaisters
         On sic a day!

14

But hark! the tent has chang'd its voice;
  There's peace an' rest nae langer;
For a' the real judges rise,
  They canna sit for anger:
Smith opens out his cauld harangues,
  On practice and on morals;
An' aff the godly pour in thrangs,
  To gie the jars an' barrels
         A lift that day.

15

What signifies his barren shine,
    Of moral pow'rs an' reason?
His English style, an' gesture fine
    Are a' clean out o' season.
Like Socrates or Antonine,
    Or some auld pagan heathen,
The moral man he does define,
    But ne'er a word o' faith in
              That's right that day.

16

In guid time comes an antidote
    Against sic poison'd nostrum;
river's mouth   For Peebles, frae the water-fit,
    Ascends the holy rostrum:
See, up he's got the word o' God,
    An' meek an' mim has view'd it,
While Common-sense has taen the road,
    An' aff, an' up the Cowgat
              Fast, fast that day.

17

next   Wee Miller niest, the guard relieves,
recites by rote   An' orthodoxy raibles,
Tho' in his heart he weel believes,
    An' thinks it auld wives' fables:
fellow; living   But faith! the birkie wants a manse:
humbugs   So, cannilie he hums them;
Altho' his carnal wit an' sense
Nearly half   Like hafflins-wise o'ercomes him
              At times that day.

18

Now butt an' ben the change-house fills,　　　tavern
　　Wi' yill-caup commentators;　　　ale-cup
Here's crying out for bakes an' gills,　　　biscuits
　　An' there the pint-stowp clatters;
While thick an' thrang, an' loud an' lang,
　　Wi' logic an' wi' Scripture,
They raise a din, that in the end
　　Is like to breed a rupture
　　　　　O' wrath that day.

19

Leeze me on drink! it gies us mair　　　Blessings
　　Than either school or college;
It kindles wit, it waukens lear,　　　learning
　　It pangs us fou o' knowledge:　　　crams
Be't whisky-gill or penny wheep,　　　small beer
　　Or onie stronger potion,
It never fails, on drinkin deep,
　　To kittle up our notion,　　　tickle
　　　　　By night or day.

20

The lads an' lasses, blythely bent
　　To mind baith saul an' body,
Sit round the table, weel content,
　　An' steer about the toddy:　　　stir
On this ane's dress, an' that ane's leuk,
　　They're makin observations;
　　While some are cozie i' the neuk,　　　corner
　　An' formin assignations
　　　　　To meet some day.

21

sounds

roaring

But now the Lord's ain trumpet touts,
    Till a' the hills are rairin,
And echoes back return the shouts;
    Black Russell is na spairin:
His piercin words, like Highlan' swords,
    Divide the joints an' marrow;
His talk o' Hell, whare devils dwell,
    Our vera 'sauls does harrow'
                Wi' fright that day!

22

full; flaming

A vast, unbottom'd, boundless pit,
    Fill'd fou o' lowin brunstane,
Whase ragin flame, an' scorchin heat,
    Wad melt the hardest whun-stane!
The half-asleep start up wi' fear,
    An' think they hear it roarin;
When presently it does appear,
    'Twas but some neebor snorin
                Asleep that day.

23

'Twad be owre lang a tale to tell,
    How monie stories past;

full portions

An' how they crouded to the yill,
    When they were a' dismist;
How drink gaed round, in cogs an' caups,
    Amang the furms an' benches;
An' cheese an' bread, frae women's laps,
    Was dealt about in lunches,

lumps

                An' dawds that day.

24

In comes a gawsie, gash guidwife,   jolly
  An' sits down by the fire,
Syne draws her kebbuck an' her knife;   Then; cheese
  The lasses they are shyer:
The auld guidmen, about the grace,
  Frae side to side they bother;
Till some ane by his bonnet lays,
  An' gies them't, like a tether,   rope
        Fu' lang that day.

25

Waesucks! for him that gets nae lass,   Alas!
  Or lasses that hae naething!
Sma' need has he to say a grace,
  Or melvie his braw claithing!   meal-dust
O wives, be mindfu', ance yoursel,
  How bonie lads ye wanted;
An' dinna for a kebbuck-heel
  Let lasses be affronted
        On sic a day!

26

Now Clinkumbell, wi' rattlin tow,   the bell-ringer; rope
  Begins to jow an' croon;   swing and toll
Some swagger hame the best they dow,   can
  Some wait the afternoon.
At slaps the billies halt a blink,   openings; fellows; bit
  Till lasses strip their shoon: take off
Wi' faith an hope, an' love an' drink,
  They're a' in famous tune
        For crack that day.   talk

27

How monie hearts this day converts
    O' sinners and o' lasses!
by nightfall; gone   Their hearts o' stane, gin night, are gane
    As saft as onie flesh is:
There's some are fou o' love divine;
    There's some are fou o' brandy;
An' monie jobs that day begin,
fornication   May end in houghmagandie
        Some ither day.

Address to the Deil

Prince! O Chief of many thronèd pow'rs!
That led th' embattl'd seraphim to war.
                    MILTON

1

O Thou! whatever title suit thee –
Hoofie   Auld Hornie, Satan, Nick, or Clootie –
Wha in yon cavern grim an' sootie,
        Clos'd under the hatches,
Splashes; dish   Spairges about the brunstane cootie,
scald   To scaud poor wretches!

2

Hear me, Auld Hangie, for a wee,   Hangman
    An' let poor damnèd bodies be;
I'm sure sma' pleasure it can gie,
        Ev'n to a deil,
To skelp an' scaud poor dogs like me   spank; scald
        An' hear us squeel.

3

Great is thy pow'r an' great thy fame;
Far kend an' noted is thy name;
An' tho' yon lowin heugh's thy hame,   flaming hollow
        Thou travels far;
An' faith! thou's neither lag, nor lame,   backward
        Nor blate, nor scaur.   bashful; afraid

4

Whyles, ranging like a roarin lion,   Now
For prey, a' holes an' corners trying;
Whyles, on the strong-wing'd tempest flyin,
        Tirlin the kirks;   Stripping
Whyles, in the human bosom pryin,
        Unseen thou lurks.

5

I've heard my rev'rend graunie say,
In lanely glens ye like to stray;
Or, where auld ruin'd castles grey
        Nod to the moon,
Ye fright the nightly wand'rer's way
        Wi' eldritch croon.

6

When twilight did my graunie summon,
To say her pray'rs, douce, honest woman!
Aft yont the dyke she's heard you bummin,
   Wi' eerie drone;
Or, rustlin, thro' the boortrees comin,
   Wi' heavy groan.

7

Ae dreary, windy, winter night,
The stars shot down wi' sklentin light,
Wi' you mysel, I gat a fright:
   Ayont the lough
Ye, like a rash-buss, stood in sight,
   Wi' waving sugh.

8

The cudgel in my nieve did shake,
Each bristl'd hair stood like a stake;
When wi' an eldritch, stoor 'quaick, quaick,'
   Amang the springs,
Awa ye squatter'd like a drake,
   On whistling wings.

9

Let warlocks grim, an' wither'd hags,
Tell how wi' you, on ragweed nags,
They skim the muirs an' dizzy crags,
   Wi' wicked speed;
And in kirk-yards renew their leagues,
   Owre howkit dead.

Margin glosses:
- sedate
- beyond
- alders
- squinting
- pond
- clump of rushes
- moan
- fist
- harsh
- ragwort
- dug-up

65

10

Thence, countra wives, wi' toil an' pain,
May plunge an' plunge the kirn in vain;   churn
For O! the yellow treasure's taen
       By witching skill;
An' dawtit, twal-pint hawkie's gaen   petted, 12-pint cow;
         As yell's the bill.   gone
                                dry as; bull

11

Thence, mystic knots mak great abuse
On young guidmen, fond, keen an' croose;   husbands;
       When the best wark-lume i' the house,   cocksure
         By cantraip wit,   tool
Is instant made no worth a louse,   magic
         Just at the bit.   nick of time

12

When thowes dissolve the snawy hoord.   hoard
An' float the jinglin icy boord,   surface
Then, water-kelpies haunt the foord,
       By your direction,
An' nighted trav'llers are allur'd
         To their destruction.

13

And aft your moss-traversing spunkies   bog; jack-o'-
Decoy the wight that late an' drunk is: lanthorns
Then bleezin, curst, mischievous monkies
       Delude his eyes,
Till in some miry slough he sunk is,
        Ne'er mair to rise.

14

When Masons' mystic word an' grip
In storms an' tempests raise you up,
must   Some cock or cat your rage maun stop,
          Or, strange to tell!
The youngest brother ye wad whip
straight   Aff straught to hell.

15

garden   Lang syne in Eden's bonie yard,
When youthfu' lovers first were pair'd,
An' all the soul of love they shar'd,
          The raptur'd hour,
Sweet on the fragrant flow'ry swaird,
          In shady bow'r.

16

scheming   Then you, ye auld, snick-drawing dog!
Ye cam to Paradise incog,
trick   An' play'd on man a cursèd brogue
          (Black be your fa'!),
shake   An' gied the infant warld a shog,
          'Maist ruin'd a'.

17

flurry   D'ye mind that day when in a bizz
smoky;   Wi' reekit duds, an' reestit gizz
scorched wig
smutty face   Ye did present your smoutie phiz
          'Mang better folk;
squinted   An' sklented on the man of Uzz
          Your spitefu' joke?

18

An' how ye gat him i' your thrall,
An' brak him out o' house an' hal',
While scabs an' botches did him gall,   *blotches*
       Wi' bitter claw;
An' lows'd his ill-tongu'd wicked scaul –   *loosed; scold*
       Was warst ava?   *of all*

19

But a' your doings to rehearse,
Your wily snares an' fechtin fierce,   *fighting*
Sin' that day Michael did you pierce
       Down to this time,
Wad ding a Lallan tongue, or Erse,   *beat; Lowland*
       In prose or rhyme.

20

An' now, Auld Cloots, I ken ye're thinkin,   *Hoofs*
A certain Bardie's rantin, drinkin,   *roistering*
Some luckless hour will send him linkin,   *hurrying*
       To your black Pit;
But, faith! he'll turn a corner jinkin,   *dodging*
       An' cheat you yet.

21

But fare-you-weel, Auld Nickie-Ben!
O' wad ye tak a thought an' men'!
Ye aiblins might – I dinna ken –   *perhaps*
       Still hae a stake:
I'm wae to think upo' yon den,   *sad*
       Ev'n for your sake!

The Death and Dying Words
of Poor Mailie

THE AUTHOR'S ONLY PET YOWE: AN UNCO
MOURNFU' TALE

together	As Mailie, an' her lambs thegither,
one	Was ae day nibblin on the tether,
hoof; looped	Upon her cloot she coost a hitch,
floundered	An' owre she warsl'd in the ditch:
	There, groanin, dying, she did lie,
doddering	When Hughoc he cam doytin by.

staring	Wi' glowrin een, an' lifted han's
	Poor Hughoc like a statue stan's;
	He saw her days were near-hand ended,
woe	But, wae's my heart! he could na mend it!
	He gapèd wide, but naething spak.
	At length poor Mailie silence brak: –

'O thou, whase lamentable face
Appears to mourn my woefu' case!
My dying words attentive hear,
An' bear them to my Master dear.

own	'Tell him, if e'er again he keep
much money	As muckle gear as buy a sheep –
	O, bid him never tie them mair,
	Wi' wicked strings o' hemp or hair!
drive	But ca' them out to park or hill,
	An' let them wander at their will:

69

So may his flock increase, an' grow
To scores o' lambs, an' packs o' woo'!

'Tell him, he was a Master kin',
An' ay was guid to me an' mine;
An' now my dying charge I gie him,
My helpless lambs, I trust them wi' him.

'O, bid him save their harmless lives,
Frae dogs, an' tods, an' butchers' knives!   *foxes*
But gie them guid cow-milk their fill,
Till they be fit to fend themsel;   *look after*
An' tent them duly, e'en an' morn,   *tend*
Wi' teats o' hay an' ripps o' corn.   *small quantities; handfuls*

'An' may they never learn the gaets,   *ways*
Of ither vile, wanrestfu' pets –   *restless*
To slink thro' slaps, an' reave an' steal,   *breaches*
At stacks o' pease, or stocks o' kail!   *plants*
So may they, like their great forbears,   *ancestors*
For monie a year come thro' the sheers: *weep*
So wives will gie them bits o' bread,
An' bairns greet for them when they're dead.

'My poor toop-lamb, my son an' heir,   *tup*
O, bid him breed him up wi' care!   *conduct*
An' if he live to be a beast,   *will not*
To pit some havins in his breast!   *ewes*
An' warn him – what I winna name –
To stay content wi' yowes at hame;
An' no to rin an' wear his cloots,

unmannerly   Like other menseless, graceless brutes.
ewekin;   ' An' niest, my yowie, silly thing;
helpless
               Gude keep thee frae a tether string!
make friends   O, may thou ne'er forgather up,
               Wi' onie blastit, moorland toop;
nibble;   But ay keep mind to moop an' mell,
meddle
               Wi' sheep o' credit like thysel!

      ' And now, my bairns, wi' my last breath,
               I lea'e my blessin wi' you baith:
               An' when you think upo' your mither,
               Mind to be kind to ane anither.

      'Now, honest Hughoc, dinna fail,
               To tell my master a' my tale;
               An' bid him burn this cursèd tether,
bladder   An' for they pains thou 'se get my blether.'

      This sad, poor Mailie turn'd her head,
eyes   An' clos'd her een amang the dead!

Epistle to James Smith

Friendship, mysterious cement of the soul!
Sweet'ner of Life, and solder of Society!
I owe thee much –

                                        BLAIR

1

Dear Smith, the slee'st, pawkie thief,   artful
That e'er attempted stealth or rief!   plunder
Ye surely hae some warlock-breef   wizard-spell
        Owre human hearts;
For ne'er a bosom yet was prief   proof
        Against your arts.

2

  For me, I swear by sun an' moon,
And ev'ry star that blinks aboon,
Ye've cost me twenty pair o' shoon,
        Just gaun to see you;
And ev'ry ither pair that's done,
        Mair taen I'm wi' you.

3

That auld, capricious carlin, Nature,   gossip
To mak amends for scrimpit stature,   stunted
She's turn'd you off, a human-creature
        On her first plan;
And in her freaks, on ev'ry feature
        She's wrote the Man.

4

Just now I've taen the fit o' rhyme,
seething brain   My barmie noodle 's working prime,
My fancy yerkit up sublime,
       Wi' hasty summon:
Hae ye a leisure-moment's time
       To hear what's comin?

5

Some rhyme a neebor's name to lash;
talk   Some rhyme (vain thought!) for needfu' cash;
Some rhyme to court the countra clash,
       An' raise a din;
trouble about   For me, an aim I never fash;
       I rhyme for fun.

6

The star that rules my luckless lot,
Has fated me the russet coat,
An' damn'd my fortune to the groat;
       But, in requit,
Has blest me with a random-shot
       O' countra wit.

7

turn   This while my notion's taen a sklent,
To try my fate in guid, black prent;
But still the mair I'm that way bent,
Softly!   Something cries, 'Hoolie!
heed   I red you, honest man, tak tent!
       Ye'll shaw your folly:

8

'There's ither poets, much your betters,
Far seen in Greek, deep men o' letters,
Hae thought they had ensur'd their debtors,
    A' future ages;
Now moths deform, in shapeless tatters,
    Their unknown pages.'

9

Then farewell hopes o' laurel-boughs
To garland my poetic brows!
Henceforth I'll rove where busy ploughs
    Are whistling thrang;   *at work*
An' teach the lanely heights an' howes   *hollows*
    My rustic sang.

10

I'll wander on, wi' tentless heed   *careless*
How never-halting moments speed,
Till Fate shall snap the brittle thread;
    Then, all unknown,
I'll lay me with th' inglorious dead,
    Forgot and gone!

11

But why o' death begin a tale?
Just now we're living sound an' hale;   *well*
Then top and maintop crowd the sail,
    Heave Care o'er-side!
And large, before Enjoyment's gale,
    Let's tak the tide.

12

This life, sae far's I understand,
Is a' enchanted fairy-land,
Where Pleasure is the magic-wand,
            That, wielded right,
Maks hours like minutes, hand in hand,
            Dance by fu' light.

13

The magic-wand then let us wield;
climbed   For, ance that five-an'-forty's speel'd,
Old age   See, crazy, weary, joyless Eild,
            Wi' wrinkl'd face,
coughing   Comes hostin, hirplin owre the field,
limping   Wi' creepin pace.

14

twilight   When ance life's day draws near the gloamin,
Then fareweel vacant, careless roamin;
An' fareweel chearfu' tankards foamin,
            An' social noise:
An' fareweel dear, deluding Woman,
            The joy of joys!

15

O Life! how pleasant, in thy morning,
Young Fancy's rays the hills adorning!
Cold-pausing Caution's lesson scorning,
            We frisk away,
Like school-boys, at th' expected warning,
            To joy an' play.

16

We wander there, we wander here,
We eye the rose upon the brier,
Unmindful that the thorn is near,
        Among the leaves;
And tho' the puny wound appear,
        Short while it grieves.

17

Some, lucky, find a flow'ry spot,
For which they never toil'd nor swat;   *sweated*
They drink the sweet and eat the fat,
        But care or pain;   *without*
And haply eye the barren hut
        With high disdain.

18

With steady aim, some fortune chase;
Keen Hope does ev'ry sinew brace;
Thro' fair, thro' foul, they urge the race,
        And seize the prey:
Then cannie, in some cozie place,   *quiet; snug*
        They close the day.

19

And others like your humble servan',
Poor wights! nae rules nor roads observin,
To right or left eternal swervin,
        They zig-zag on;
Till, curst with age, obscure an' starvin,
        They aften groan.

20

Alas! What bitter toil an' straining –
But truce with peevish, poor complaining!
Is Fortune's fickle *Luna* waning?
    E'en let her gang!
Beneath what light she has remaining,
      Let's sing our sang.

21

My pen I here fling to the door,
And kneel, ye Pow'rs! and warm implore,
'Tho' I should wander *Terra* o'er,
    In all her climes,
Grant me but this, I ask no more,
plenty   Ay rowth o' rhymes.

22

dripping 'Gie dreeping roasts to countra lairds,
Till icicles hing frae their beards;
clothes   Gie fine braw claes to fine life-guards
      And maids of honor;
ale   And yill an' whisky gie to cairds,
sicken   Until they sconner.

23

'A title, Dempster merits it;
A garter gie to Willie Pitt;
Gie wealth to some be-ledger'd cit,
    In cent. per cent.;
But give me real, sterling wit,
      And I'm content.

24

'While ye are pleas'd to keep me hale,
I'll sit down o'er my scanty meal,
Be't water-brose or muslin-kail,
   Wi' cheerfu' face,
As lang's the Muses dinna fail
    To say the grace.'

meal and water; beefless broth

25

An anxious e'e I never throws
Behint my lug, or by my nose;
I jouk beneath Misfortune's blows
   As weel's I may;
Sworn foe to sorrow, care, and prose,
    I rhyme away.

ear
duck

26

O ye douce folk that live by rule,
Grave, tideless-blooded, calm an' cool,
Compar'd wi' you – O fool! fool! fool!
   How much unlike!
Your hearts are just a standing pool,
    Your lives a dyke!

sedate

wall

27

Nae hair-brained, sentimental traces
In your unletter'd, nameless faces!
In *arioso* trills and graces
   Ye never stray;
But *gravissimo*, solemn, basses
    Ye hum away.

28

Ye are sae grave, nae doubt ye 're wise;
Nae ferly tho' ye do despise
The hairum-scairum, ram-stam boys,
                    The rattling sqad:
I see ye upward cast your eyes –
                    Ye ken the road!

marvel
headlong

29

Whilst I – but I shall haud me there,
Wi' you I 'll scarce gang onie where –
Then, Jamie, I shall say nae mair,
                    But quat my sang.
Content wi' you to mak a pair,
                    Whare'er I gang.

hold

quit

The Vision

DUAN FIRST

1

The sun had clos'd the winter day,
The curlers quat their roaring play,   *ceased*
And hunger'd maukin taen her way,   *hare*
        To kail-yards green,   *kitchen gardens*
While faithless snaws ilk step betray   *each*
        Whare she has been.

2

The thresher's weary flingin-tree,   *flail*
The lee-lang day had tired me;   *live-long*
And when the day had clos'd his e'e
        Far i' the west,
Ben i' the spence, right pensivelie,   *Back; parlour*
        I gaed to rest.   *went*

3

There, lanely by the ingle-cheek,   *-side*
I sat and ey'd the spewing reek,   *volleying*
That fill'd, wi hoast-provoking smeek,   *cough-; drift*
        The auld clay biggin;   *structure*
An' heard the restless rattons squeak   *rats*
        About the riggin.   *rooftree*

4

dusty	All in this mottie, misty clime,
	I backward mus'd on wasted time:
	How I had spent my youthfu' prime,
	An' done naething,
nonsense	But stringing blethers up in rhyme,
	For fools to sing.

5

Had I to guid advice but harkit,
I might, by this, hae led a market,
Or strutted in a bank and clarkit
      My cash-account:
-shirted   While here, half-mad, half-fed, half-sarkit,
      Is a' th' amount.

6

weakling   I started, mutt'ring 'Blockhead! coof!'
horny palm   An' heav'd on high my waukit loof,
To swear by a' yon starry roof,
      Or some rash aith,
That I henceforth would be rhyme-proof
      Till my last breath –

7

latch   When click! the string the snick did draw;
And jee! the door gaed to the wa';
-flame   And by my ingle-lowe I saw,
      Now bleezin bright,
young woman   A tight, outlandish hizzie, braw,
      Come full in sight.

81

8

Ye need na doubt, I held my whisht;   *peace*
The infant aith, half-form'd, was crusht;
I glowr'd as eerie's I'd been dusht,   *stared; touched*
      In some wild glen;
When sweet, like modest Worth, she blusht,   *inside*
      And steppèd ben.

9

Green, slender, leaf-clad holly-boughs
Were twisted, gracefu', round her brows;
I took her for some Scottish Muse,
      By that same token;
And come to stop those reckless vows,
      Would soon been broken.

10

A 'hair-brain'd' sentimental trace'
Was strongly markèd in her face;
A wildly-witty, rustic grace
      Shone full upon her;
Her eye, ev'n turn'd on empty space,
      Beam'd keen with honor.

11

Down flow'd her robe, a tartan sheen,   *bright*
Till half a leg was scrimply seen;   *barely*
And such a leg! my bonie Jean
      Could only peer it;
Sae straught, sae taper, tight an' clean   *straight*
      Nane else came near it.

12

Her mantle large, of greenish hue,
My gazing wonder chiefly drew;
Deep lights and shades, bold-mingling, threw
    A lustre grand;
And seem'd, to my astonish'd view,
    A well-known land.

13

Here, rivers in the sea were lost;
There, mountains to the skies were toss't;
Here, tumbling billows mark'd the coast
    With surging foam;
There, distant shone Art's lofty boast,
    The lordly dome.

14

Here, Doon pour'd down his far-fetch'd floods;
There, well-fed Irwine stately thuds:
Auld hermit Ayr staw thro' his woods,
    On to the shore;
And many a lesser torrent scuds
    With seeming roar.

beats
stole

15

Low, in a sandy valley spread,
An ancient borough rear'd her head;
Still, as in Scottish story read,
    She boasts a race
To ev'ry nobler virtue bred,
    And polish'd grace.

16

By stately tow'r, or palace fair,
Or ruins pendent in the air,
Bold stems of heroes, here and there,
   I could discern;
Some seem'd to muse, some seem'd to dare
   With feature stern.

17

My heart did glowing transport feel,
To see a race heroic wheel,
And brandish round the deep-dyed steel
   In sturdy blows;
While, back-recoiling, seem'd to reel
   Their suthron foes.

18

His Country's Saviour, mark him well!
Bold Richardton's heroic swell;
The chief, on Sark who glorious fell
   In high command;
And he whom ruthless fates expel
   His native land.

19

There, where a sceptr'd Pictish shade
Stalk'd round his ashes lowly laid,
I mark'd a martial race, pourtray'd
   In colours strong:
Bold, soldier-featur'd, undismay'd,
   They strode along.

20

Thro' many a wild, romanitc grove,
Near many a hermit-fancied cove
(Fit haunts for friendship or for love
      In musing mood),
An aged Judge, I saw him rove,
      Dispensing good.

21

With deep-struck, reverential awe,
The learned Sire and Son I saw:
To Nature's God, and nature's law,
      They gave their lore;
This, all its source and end to draw,
      That, to adore.

22

Brydon's brave ward I well could spy,
Beneath old Scotia's smiling eye;
Who call'd on Fame, low standing by
      To hand him on,
Where many a patriot-name on high,
      And hero shone.

DUAN SECOND

1

With musing-deep, astonish'd stare,
I view'd the heavenly-seeming Fair;
A whisp'ring throb did witness bear
      Of kindred sweet,
When with an elder sister's air
      She did me greet.

2

'All hail! my own inspirèd Bard!
In me thy native Muse regard!
Nor longer mourn thy fate is hard,
        Thus poorly low!
I come to give thee such reward,
        As we bestow.

3

'Know, the great Genius of this land
Has many a light aerial band,
Who, all beneath his high command,
        Harmoniously,
As arts or arms they understand,
        Their labors ply.

4

'They Scotia's race among them share:
Some fire the soldier on to dare;
Some rouse the patriot up to bare
        Corruption's heart;
Some teach the bard – a darling care –
        The tuneful art.

5

' 'Mong swelling floods of reeking gore,
They, ardent, kindling spirits pour;
Or, 'mid the venal Senate's roar,
        They, sightless, stand,
To mend the honest patriot-lore,
        And grace the hand.

6

'And when the bard, or hoary sage,
Charm or instruct the future age,
They bind the wild poetic rage
      In energy;
Or point the inconclusive page
      Full on the eye.

7

'Hence, Fullarton, the brave and young;
Hence, Dempster's zeal-inspirèd tongue;
Hence, sweet, harmonious Beattie sung
      His *Minstrel* lays,
Or tore, with noble ardour stung,
      The sceptic's bays.

8

'To lower orders are assign'd
The humbler ranks of human-kind,
The rustic bard, the laboring hind,
      The artisan;
All chuse, as various they're inclin'd,
      The various man.

9

'When yellow waves the heavy grain,
The threat'ning storm some strongly rein,
Some teach to meliorate the plain,
      With tillage-skill;
And some instruct the shepherd-train,
      Blythe o'er the hill.

10

'Some hint the lover's harmless wile;
Some grace the maiden's artless smile;
Some soothe the laborer's weary toil
      For humble gains,
And make his cottage-scenes beguile
      His cares and pains.

11

'Some, bounded to a district-space,
Explore at large man's infant race,
To mark the embryotic trace
      Of rustic bard;
And careful note each opening grace,
      A guide and guard.

12

'Of these am I – Coila my name;
And this district as mine I claim,
Where once the Campbells, chiefs of fame,
      Held ruling pow'r:
I mark'd thy embryo-tuneful flame,
      Thy natal hour.

13

'With future hope I oft would gaze,
Fond, on thy little early ways:
Thy rudely caroll'd, chiming phrase,
      In uncouth rhymes;
Fir'd at the simple, artless lays
      Of other times.

14

'I saw thee seek the sounding shore,
Delighted with the dashing roar;
Or when the North his fleecy store
      Drove thro' the sky,
I saw grim Nature's visage hoar
      Struck thy young eye.

15

'Or when the deep green-mantled earth
Warm cherish'd ev'ry flow'ret's birth,
And joy and music pouring forth
      In ev'ry grove;
I saw thee eye the gen'ral mirth
      With boundless love.

16

'When ripen'd fields and azure skies
Call'd forth the reapers' rustling noise,
I saw thee leave their ev'ning joys,
      And lonely stalk,
To vent thy bosom's swelling rise,
      In pensive walk.

17

'When youthful Love, warm-blushing, strong,
Keen-shivering, shot thy nerves along,
Those accents grateful to thy tongue,
      Th' adorèd *Name*,
I taught thee how to pour in song
      To soothe thy flame.

18

'I saw thy pulse's maddening play,
Wild-send thee Pleasure's devious way,
Misled by Fancy's meteor-ray,
      By passion driven;
But yet the light that led astray
      Was light from Heaven.

19

'I taught thy manners-painting strains
The loves, the ways of simple swains,
Till now, o'er all my wide domains
      Thy fame extends;
And some, the pride of Coila's plains,
      Become thy friends.

20

'Thou canst not learn, nor can I show,
To paint with Thomson's landscape glow;
Or wake the bosom-melting throe
      With Shenstone's art;
Or pour, with Gray, the moving flow
      Warm on the heart.

21

'Yet, all beneath th' unrivall'd rose,
The lowly daisy sweetly blows;
Tho' large the forest's monarch throws
      His army-shade,
Yet green the juicy hawthorn grows
      Adown the glade.

22

'Then never murmur nor repine;
Strive in thy humble sphere to shine;
And trust me, not Potosi's mine,
   Nor king's regard,
Can give a bliss o'ermatching thine,
   A rustic Bard.

23

'To give my counsels all in one:
Thy tuneful flame still careful fan;
Preserve the dignity of Man,
   With soul erect;
And trust the Universal Plan
   Will all protect.

24

'And wear thou *this*.' She solemn said,
And bound the holly round my head:
The polish'd leaves and berries red
   Did rustling play;
And, like a passing thought, she fled
   In light away.

The Cotter's Saturday Night

INSCRIBED TO R. AIKEN, ESQ.

Let not Ambition mock their useful toil,
Their homely joys, and destiny obscure;
Nor Grandeur hear, with a disdainful smile,
The short and simple annals of the poor.

GRAY

1

My lov'd, my honor'd, much respected friend!
    No mercenary bard his homage pays;
With honest pride, I scorn each selfish end,
    My dearest meed, a friend's esteem and praise:
    To you I sing, in simple Scottish lays,
The lowly train in life's sequester'd scene;
    The native feelings strong, the guileless ways;
What Aiken in a cottage would have been;
Ah! tho' his worth unknown, far happier there I ween!

2

November chill blaws loud wi' angry sugh;   wail
    The short'ning winter-day is near a close;
The miry beasts retreating frae the pleugh;
    The black'ning trains o' craws to their repose:
    The toil-worn Cotter frae his labor goes –
This night his weekly moil is at an end,
    Collects his spades, his mattocks, and his hoes,
Hoping the morn in ease and rest to spend,

And weary, o'er the moor, his course does
      hameward bend.

3

At length his lonely cot appears in view,
    Beneath the shelter of an aged tree;
totter   Th' expectant wee-things, toddlin, stacher through
fluttering   To meet their dad, wi' flichterin' noise and glee.
His wee bit ingle, blinkin bonilie,
    His clean hearth-stane, his thrifty wifie's smile
The lisping infant, prattling on his knee,
    Does a' his weary carking cares beguile,
And makes him quite forget his labor and his toil.

4

By and bye Belyve, the elder bairns come drapping in,
    At service out, amang the farmers roun';
follow; Some ca' the pleugh, some herd, some tentie rin
heedful run
quiet   A cannie errand to a neebor town:
Their eldest hope, their Jenny, woman grown,
    In youthfu' bloom, love sparkling in her e'e,
Comes hame; perhaps, to shew a braw new gown,
hard-; wages   Or deposite her sair-won penny-fee,
To help her parents dear, if they in hardship be.

5

With joy unfeign'd, brothers and sisters meet,
asks   And each for other's weelfare kindly spiers:
The social hours, swift-wing'd, unnotic'd fleet;
wonders   Each tells the uncos that he sees or hears.
The parents partial eye their hopeful years;
    Anticipation forward points the view;

The mother, wi' her needle and her sheers,
Gars auld claes look amaist as weel's the new;   Makes; clothes
The father mixes a' wi' admonition due.

6

Their master's and their mistress's command
     The younkers a' are warned to obey;
And mind their labors wi' an eydent hand,   diligent
     And ne'er, tho' out o' sight, to jauk or play: trifle
'And O! be sure to fear the Lord alway,
     And mind your duty, duly, morn and night;
     Lest in temptation's path ye gang astray,
Implore His counsel and assisting might:
They never sought in vain that sought the Lord
          aright.'

But hark! a rap comes gently to the door;
     Jenny, wha kens the meaning o' the same,
Tells how a neebor lad came o'er the moor,
     To do some errands, and convoy her hame.
     The wily mother sees the conscious flame
Sparkle in Jenny's e'e, and flush her cheek;
     With heart-struck anxious care, enquires his
          name,
While Jenny hafflins is afraid to speak;   half
Weel-pleas'd the mother hears, it's nae wild,
          worthless rake.

8

With kindly welcome, Jenny brings him ben;
     A strappin' youth, he takes the mother's eye;   inside

Blythe Jenny sees the visit's no ill taen;
    The father cracks of horses, pleughs, and kye.
The youngster's artless heart o'erflows wi' joy,
    But blate and laithfu', scarce can weel behave;
    The mother, wi' a woman's wiles, can spy
What makes the youth sae bashfu' and sae grave;
    Weel-pleas'd to think her bairn's respected like the
        lave.

chats; cattle (margin)
shy; sheepish (margin)
rest (margin)

9

O happy love! where love like this is found:
    O heart-felt raptures! bliss beyond compare!
I've pacèd much this weary, mortal round,
    And sage experience bids me thus declare:–
    'If Heaven a draught of heavenly pleasure spare,
One cordial in this melancholy vale,
    'Tis when a youthful, loving, modest pair,
In other's arms, breathe out the tender tale
Beneath the milk-white thorn that scents the ev'ning
        gale.'

10

Is there, in human form, that bears a heart,
    A wretch! a villain! lost to love and truth!
That can, with studied, sly, ensnaring art,
    Betray sweet Jenny's unsuspecting youth?
    Curse on his perjur'd arts! dissembling, smooth!
Are honor, virtue, conscience, all exil'd?
    Is there no pity, no relenting ruth,
Points to the parents fondling o'er their child?
Then paints the ruin'd maid, and their distraction
        wild?

compassion (margin)

11

But now the supper crowns their simple board,
    The healsome parritch, chief o' Scotia's food;   *wholesome porridge*
The soupe their only hawkie does afford,   *milk; cow*
    That, 'yont the hallan snugly chows her cood;   *beyond; wall*
    The dame brings forth, in complimental mood,
To grace the lad, her weel-hain'd kebbuck, fell;   *-saved cheese; pungent*
    And aft he's prest, and aft he ca's it guid;
The frugal wifie, garrulous, will tell,
How 'twas a towmond auld, sin' lint was i' the bell.   *12–month; flax; flower*

12

The chearfu' supper done, wi' serious face,
    They, round the ingle, form a circle wide;
The sire turns o'er, wi' patriarchal grace,
    The big ha'-Bible, ance his father's pride.
    His bonnet rev'rently is laid aside,
His lyart haffets wearing thin and bare;   *grey side-locks*
    Those strains that once did sweet in Zion glide,
He wales a portion with judicious care,   *selects*
And 'Let us worship God!' he says, with solemn air.

13

They chant their artless notes in simple guise,
    They tune their hearts, by far the noblest aim;
Perhaps *Dundee's* wild-warbling measures rise;
    Or plaintive *Martyrs*, worthy of the name;
    Or noble *Elgin* beets the heaven-ward flame,   *fans*
The sweetest far of Scotia's holy lays:
    Compar'd with these, Italian trills are tame;
The tickl'd ears no heart-felt raptures raise;
Nae unison hae they, with our Creator's praise.

14

The priest-like father reads the sacred page,
  How Abram was the friend of God on high;
Or, Moses bade eternal warfare wage
  With Amalek's ungracious progeny;
  Or, how the royal Bard did groaning lie
Beneath the stroke of Heaven's avenging ire;
  Or Job's pathetic plaint, and wailing cry;
Or rapt Isaiah's wild, seraphic fire;
Or other holy Seers that tune the sacred lyre.

15

Perhaps the Christian volume is the theme:
  How guiltless blood for guilty man was shed;
How He, who bore in Heaven the second name,
  Had not on earth whereon to lay His head;
  How His first followers and servants sped;
The precepts sage they wrote to many a land;
  How he, who lone in Patmos banishèd,
Saw in the sun a mighty angel stand,
And heard great Bab'lon's doom pronounc'd by
        Heaven's command.

16

Then kneeling down to Heaven's Eternal King,
  The saint, the father, and the husband prays:
Hope 'springs exulting on triumphant wing.'
  That thus they all shall meet in future days,
  There, ever bask in uncreated rays,
No more to sigh or shed the bitter tear,
  Together hymning their Creator's praise,
In such society, yet still more dear;
While circling time moves round in an eternal
        sphere.

97

17

Compar'd with this, how poor Religion's pride,
    In all the pomp of method, and of art;
When men display to congregations wide
    Devotion's ev'ry grace, except the heart!
    The Power, incens'd, the pageant will desert,
    The pompous strain, the sacerdotal stole:
    But haply, in some cottage far apart,
May hear, well-pleas'd, the language of the soul,
And in His Book of Life the inmates poor enroll.

18

Then homeward all take off their sev'ral way;
    The youngling cottagers retire to rest:
The parent-pair their secret homage pay,
    And proffer up to Heaven the warm request.
    That He who stills the raven's clam'rous nest,
And decks the lily fair in flow'ry pride,
    Would, in the way His wisdom sees the best,
For them and for their little ones provide;
But, chiefly, in their hearts with Grace Divine preside.

19

From scenes like these, old Scotia's grandeur springs
    That makes her lov'd at home, rever'd abroad:
Princes and lords are but the breath of kings,
    'An honest man's the noble(st) work of God';
    And certes, in fair Virtue's heavenly road,
The cottage leaves the palace far behind;
    What is a lordling's pomp? a cumbrous load,
Disguising oft the wretch of human kind,
Studies in arts of Hell, in wickedness refin'd!

20

O Scotia! my dear, my native soil!
  For whom my warmest wish to Heaven is sent!
Long may the hardy sons of rustic toil
  Be blest with health, and peace, and sweet content!
  And O! may Heaven their simple lives prevent
From Luxury's contagion, weak and vile!
  Then, howe'er crowns and coronets be rent,
A virtuous populace may rise the while,
And stand a wall of fire around their much-lov'd Isle.

21

O Thou! who pour'd the patriotic tide,
  That stream'd thro' Wallace's undaunted heart,
Who dar'd to, nobly, stem tyrannic pride,
  Or nobly die, the second glorious part:
  (The patriot's God, peculiarly thou art,
His friend, inspirer, guardian, and reward!)
  O never, never Scotia's realm desert;
But still the patriot, and the patriot-bard
In bright succession raise, her ornament and guard!

To A Mouse

ON TURNING HER UP IN HER NEST WITH THE PLOUGH, NOVEMBER 1785

1

Wee, sleekit, cowrin, tim'rous beastie,   sleek
O, what a panic's in thy breastie!
Thou need na start awa sae hasty
       Wi' bickering brattle!   hurrying / scamper
I wad be laith to rin an' chase thee,   loth
       Wi' murdering pattle!   plough-staff

2

I'm truly sorry man's dominion
Has broken Nature's social union,
An' justifies that ill opinion
       Which makes thee startle
At me, thy poor, earth-born companion
       An' fellow mortal!

3

I doubt na, whyles, but thou may thieve;   sometimes
What then? poor beastie, thou maun live!
A daimen icket in a thrave   odd ear; twenty-four sheaves
       'S a sma' request;
I'll get a blessin wi' the lave,   what's left
       An' never miss't!

4

Thy wee-bit housie, too, in ruin!
Its silly wa's the win's are strewin!   feeble; winds
An' naething, now, to big a new ane,
       O' foggage green!

coarse grass
bitter

An' bleak December's win's ensuin,
Baith snell an' keen!

5

Thou saw the fields laid bare an' waste,
An' weary winter comin fast,
An' cozie here, beneath the blast,
Though thought to dwell,
Till crash! the cruel coulter past
Out thro' thy cell.

6

stubble

Without; holding

endure
hoar-frost

That wee bit heap o' leaves an' stibble,
Has cost thee monie a weary nibble!
Now thou's turned out, for a' thy trouble,
But house or hald,
To thole the winter's sleety dribble,
An' cranreuch cauld!

7

alone

askew

But Mousie, thou art no thy lane,
In proving foresight may be vain;
The best-laid schemes o' mice an' men
Gang aft agley,
An' lea'e us nought but grief an' pain,
For promis'd joy!

8

Still thou art blest, compared wi' me!
The present only toucheth thee:
But och! I backward cast my e'e,
On prospects dear!
An' forward, tho' I canna see,
I guess an' fear!

To A Mountain Daisy

ON TURNING ONE DOWN WITH THE PLOUGH IN APRIL 1786

1

Wee, modest, crimson-tippèd flow'r,
Thou's met me in an evil hour;
For I maun crush amang the stoure   dust
         Thy slender stem:
To spare thee now is past my pow'r,
         Thou bonie gem.

2

Alas! it's no thy neebor sweet,
The bonie lark, companion meet,
Bending thee 'mang the dewy weet,   wet
         Wi' spreckl'd breast!
When upward-springing, blythe, to greet
         The purpling east.

3

Cauld blew the bitter-biting north
Upon thy early, humble birth;
Yet cheerfully thou glinted forth   sparkled
         Amid the storm,
Scarce rear'd above the parent-earth
         Thy tender form.

4

The flaunting flow'rs our gardens yield,
High shelt'ring woods and wa's maun shield;   must

shelter

But thou, beneath the random bield
                    O' clod or stane,
bare stubble

Adorns the histie stibble-field,
                    Unseen, alane.

5

There, in thy scanty mantle clad,
Thy snawie bosom sun-ward spread,
Thou lifts thy unassuming head
            In humble guise;
But now the share uptears they bed,
                    And low thou lies!

6

Such is the fate of artless maid,
Sweet flow'ret of the rural shade!
By love's simplicity betray'd,
                    And guileless trust;
Till she, like thee, all soil'd, is laid
                    Low i' the dust.

7

Such is the fate of simple Bard,
On Life's rough ocean luckless starr'd!
Unskilful he to note the card
            Of prudent lore,
Till billows rage, and gales blow hard,
                    And whelm him o'er'.

8

Such fate to suffering Worth is giv'n,
Who long with sants and woes has striv'n,
By human pride or cunning driv'n

To mis'ry's brink;
Till, wrench'd of ev'ry stay but Heav'n,
He, ruin'd, sink!

9

Ev'n thou who mourn'st the Daisy's fate,
That fat is thine – no distant date;
Stern Ruin's plough-share drives elate,
Full on thy bloom,
Till crush'd beneath the furrow's weight
Shall be thy doom!

To A Louse

ON SEEING ONE ON A LADY'S BONNET AT CHURCH

1

Ha! whare ye gaun, ye crowlin ferlie?   crawling wonder
Your impudence protects you sairly,
I canna say but ye strunt rarely   swagger
          Owre gauze and lace,
Tho' faith! I fear ye dine but sparely
          On sic a place.

2

Ye ugly, creepin, blastit wonner,
Detested, shunn'd by saunt an' sinner,
foot   How daur ye set your fit upon her –
        Sae fine a lady!
Gae somewhere else and seek your dinner
        On some poor body.

3

Off! temples squat Swith! in some beggar's hauffet squattle:
scramble There ye may creep, and sprawl, and sprattle,
Wi' ither kindred, jumping cattle,
        In shoals and nations;
Whare horn nor bane ne'er daur unsettle
        Your thick plantations.

4

Now haud you there! y're out o' sight,
keep
falderals Below the fatt'rils, snug an' tight;
Na, faith ye yet! ye'll no be right,
        Till ye've got on it –
The vera tapmost, tow'ring height
        O' Miss's bonnet.

5

My sooth! right bauld yet set your nose out,
gooseberry As plump an' grey as onie grozet:
rosin O for some rank, mercurial rozet,
deadly; powder   Or fell, red smeddum,
I'd gie ye sic a hearty dose o't,
breech   Wad dress your droddum!

6

I wad na been surpris'd to spy
You on an auld wife's flainen toy;
Or aiblins some bit duddie boy,
    On's wyliecoat;
But Miss's fine Lunardi! fye!
    How daur ye do't?

would not have
flannel cap
maybe; small ragged
undervest
balloon bonnet

7

O Jenny, dinna toss your head,
An' set your beauties a' abroad!
Ye little ken what cursèd speed
    The blastie's makin!
Thae winks an' finger-ends, I dread,
    Are notice takin!

abroad

Those

8

O wad some Power the giftie gie us
To see oursels as ithers see us!
It wad frae monie a blunder free us,
    An' foolish notion:
What airs in dress an' gait wad lea'e us,
    An' ev'n devotion

Epistle to J. Lapraik

AN OLD SCOTTISH BARD, APRIL 1, 1785

1

While briers an' woodbines budding green,
partidges calling And paitricks scraichin loud at e'en,
the hare scudding An' morning poussie whiddin seen,
          Inspire my Muse,
This freedom, in an unknown frien'
          I pray excuse.

2

meeting On Fasten-e'en we had a rockin,
have a chat To ca' the crack and weave our stockin;
And there was muckle fun and jokin,
          Ye need na doubt;
set-to At length we had a hearty yokin,
          At 'sang about.'

3

one There was ae sang, amang the rest,
Above Aboon them a' it pleas'd me best,
That some kind husband had addrest
          To some sweet wife:
thrilled It thril'd the heart-strings thro' the breast,
          A' to the life.

4

I've scarce heard ought describ'd sae weel,
What gen'rous, manly bosoms feel;
Thought I, 'Can this be Pope or Steele,

107

Or Beattie's wark?'
They tauld me 'twas an odd kind chiel   chap
About Muirkirk.

5

It pat me fidgin-fain to hear't,   tingling-wild
An' sae about him there I spier't;   asked
Then a' that kent him round declar'd
He had ingine;   genius
That nane excell'd it, few cam near't,
It was sae fine:

6

That, set him to a pint of ale,
An' either douce or merry tale,   sober
Or rhymes an' sangs he'd made himsel,
Or witty catches,
'Tween Inverness an' Teviotdale,
He had few matches.

7

Then up I gat, an' swoor an aith,   swore
Tho' I should pawn my pleugh an' graith,   harness
Or die a cadger pownie's death,   hawker
At some dyke-back,   Behind a fence
A pint an' gill I'd gie them baith,
To hear your crack.   talk

8

But, first an' foremost, I should tell,
Amaist as soon as I could spell,
I to the crambo-jingle fell;   rhyming

108

Tho' rude an' rough –

humming   Yet crooning to a body's sel,

Does weel eneugh.

9

I am nae poet, in a sense;
But just a rhymer like by chance,
An' hae to learning nae pretence;
    Yet, what the matter?
Whene'er my Muse does on me glance,
    I jingle at her.

10

Your critic-folk may cock their nose,
And say, 'How can you e'er propose,
You wha ken hardly verse frae prose,
    To mak a sang?'
But, by your leaves, my learned foes,
    Ye're maybe wrang.

11

What's a' your jargon o' your Schools,
Your Latin names for horns an' stools?
If honest Nature made you fools,

serves   What sairs your grammers

stone-breaking   Ye'd better taen up spades and shools,
    Or knappin-hammers.

12

dunderheads   A set o' dull, conceited hashes
Confuse their brains in college-classes,

young bullocks   They gang in stirks, and come out asses,

> Plain truth to speak;
> An' syne they think to climb Parnassus   *then*
>   By dint o' Greek!

13

> Gie me ae spark o' Nature's fire,
> That's a' the learning I desire;
> Then, tho' I drudge thro' dub an' mire   *puddle*
>   At pleugh or cart,
> My Muse, tho' hamely in attire,
>   May touch the heart.

14

> O for a spunk o' Allan's glee,   *spark*
> Or Fergusson's, the bauld an' slee,   *sly*
> Or bright Lapraik's, my friend to be,
>   If I can hit it!
> That would be lear eneugh for me,   *learning*
>   If I could get it.

15

> Now, sir, if ye hae friends enow,
> Tho' real friends I b'lieve are few;
> Yet, if your catalogue be fow,   *full*
>   I'se no insist: *I'll*
> But, gif ye want ae friend that's true,
>   I'm on your list.

16

> I winna blaw about mysel,   *brag*
> As ill I like my fauts to tell;
> But friends, an' folks that wish me well,
>   They sometimes roose me;   *praise*

EPISTLE TO J. LAPRAIK

Tho', I maun own, as monie still
                    As far abuse me.

17

one | There's ae wee faut they whyles lay to me,
God | I like the lasses - Gude forgie me!
Coin | For monie a plack they wheedle frae me
                    At dance or fair;
Maybe some ither thing they gie me,
                    They weel can spare.

18

But Mauchline Race or Mauchline Fair,
I should be proud to meet you there:
We'll | We'se gie ae night's discharge to care,
                    If we forgather;
And hae a swap o' rhymin-ware
                    Wi' ane anither.

19

four-gill cup, | The four-gill chap, we'se gar him clatter,
we'll make |
christen; streaming | An' kirsen him wi' reekin water;
Then; draught | Syne we'll sit down an' tak our whitter,
                    To cheer our heart;
An' faith, we'se be acquainted better
                    Before we part.

20

worldly | Awa ye selfish, warly race,
manners | Wha think that havins, sense, an' grace,
Ev'n love an' friendship should give place
the hunt for coin | To Catch-the-Plack!

I dinna like to see your face,
>Nor hear your crack.

21

But ye whom social pleasure charms,
Whose hearts the tide of kindness warms,
Who hold your being on the terms,
>'Each aid the others,'
Come to my bowl, come to my arms,
>My friends, my brothers!

22

But, to conclude my lang epistle,
As my auld pen's worn to the grissle,
Twa lines frae you wad gar me fissle,   tingle
>Who am most fervent,
While I can either sing or whistle,
>Your friend and servant.

Death and Doctor Hornbook

A TRUE STORY

1

Some books are lies frae end to end,
And some great lies were never penn'd:
Ev'n ministers, they hae been kend,
>In holy rapture,

fib

> A rousing whid at times to vend,
>> And nail't wi' Scripture.

2

going

> But this that I am gaun to tell,
> Which lately on a night befel,
> Is just as true's the Deil's in hell

(in effigy)

>> Or Dublin city:
> That e'er he nearer comes oursel
>> 'S a muckle pity!

3

village ale; jolly

drunk

staggered now and then; care
clear

> The clachan yill had made me canty,
> I was na fou, but just had plenty:
> I stacher'd whyles, but yet took tent ay
>> To free the ditches;
> An' hillocks, stanes, an' bushes, kend ay
>> Frae ghaists an' witches.

4

stare

above

> The rising moon began to glowr
> The distant Cumnock Hills out-owre:
> To count her horns, wi' a' my pow'r
>> I set mysel;
> But whether she had three or four,
>> I cou'd na tell.

5

> I was come round about the hill,
> And todlin down on Willie's mill,
> Setting my staff wi' a' my skill

steady

>> To keep me sicker;

Tho' leeward whyles, against my will,
　　　　I took a bicker.

6

I there wi' *Something* does forgather;
That pat me in an eerie swither;　　　　　　put;
　　　　　　　　　　　　　　　　　ghostly dread
An awfu' scythe, out-owre ae shouther,　across one
　　　　Clear-dangling, hang;　　　　hung
A three-tae'd leister on the ither　　three-pronged
　　　　Lay, large an' lang.　　　　fish-spear

7

Its stature seem'd lang Scotch ells twa;
The queerest shape that e'er I saw,
For fient a wame it had ava;　　　　fiend; belly;
　　　　And then its shanks,　　　　at all
They were as thin, as sharp an' sma'
　　　　As cheeks o' branks.

8

'Guid-een,' quo' I; 'Friend! hae ye been mawin,
When ither folk are busy sawin?'
It seem'd to mak a kind o' stan',　　　halt
　　　　But naething spak.
At length, says I: 'Friend! whare ye gaun?　where are you
　　　　Will ye go back?'　　　　going
　　　　　　　　　　　　　　i.e. to the
　　　　　　　　　　　　　　tavern

9

It spak right howe: 'My name is Death;　hollow
But be na' fley'd.' Quoth I: 'Guid faith,
Ye're may be come to stap my breath;　scared
　　　　But tent me, billie:　　　heed; comrade

advise;
damage
large knife

I red ye weel, take care o' skaith,
   See, there's a gully!'

10

blade

'Gudeman,' quo' he, 'put up your whittle,
I'm no design'd to try its mettle;
But if I did, I wad be kittle
   To be mislear'd:
I wad na mind it, no that spittle
   Out-owre my beard.'

11

give us; agreed

'Weel, weel!' says I, 'A bargain be't;
Come, gie's your hand, an' say we're gree't;
We'll ease our shanks, an' tak a seat:
   Come, gie's your news:

road

This while ye hae been monie a gate,
   At monie a house.'

12

'Ay, ay!' quo' he, an' shook his head,
'It's e'en a lang, lang time indeed

cut

Sin' I began to nick the thread
   An' choke the breath:
Folk maun do something for their bread,
   An' sae maun Death.

13

well-nigh

'Sax thousand years are near-hand fled

butchering

Sin' I was to the butching bred,
An' monie a scheme in vain's been laid

stop; scare

   To stap or scar me;

115

Till ane Hornbook' ta'en up the trade,
    And faith! he'll waur me.   *worst*

14

'Ye ken Jock Hornbook i' the clachan?
Deil mak his king's-hood in a spleuchan! -   *scrotum;*
               tobacco pouch
He's grown sae weel acquant wi' *Buchan*
    And ither chaps,
The weans haud out their fingers laughin,   *children*
    An' pouk my hips.   *poke; buttocks*

15

'See, here's a scythe, an' there's a dart,
They hae pierc'd monie a gallant heart;
But Doctor Hornbook wi' his art
    An' cursèd skill,
Has made them baith no worth a fart,
    Damn'd haet they'll kill!   *The devil a one*

16

''Twas but yestreen, nae farther gane,   *gone*
I threw a noble throw at ane;
Wi' less, I'm sure, I've hundreds slain;
    But Deil-ma-care!
It just played dirl on the bane,   *went tinkle*
    But did nae mair.

17

'Hornbook was by wi' ready art,
An' had sae fortify'd the part,
That when I lookèd to my dart,
    It was sae blunt,

Fient haet o't wad hae pierc'd the heart

cabbage-stalk Of a kail-runt.

18

'I drew my scythe in sic a fury,

tumbled I near-hand cowpit wi' my hurry,
But yet the bauld Apothecary
        Withstood the shock:
I might as weel hae try'd a quarry
      O' hard whin-rock.

19

'Ev'n them he canna get attended,
Altho' their face he ne'er had kend it,

cabbage-leaf Just shite in a kail-blade an' send it,
        As soon's he smells't,
Baith their disease and what will mend it,
      At once he tells't.

20

knives 'And then a' doctor's saws and whittles
Of a' dimensions, shapes, an' mettles,
A' kinds o' boxes, mugs, and bottles,
        He's sure to hae;
Their Latin names as fast he rattles
      As A B C.

21

'Calces o' fossils, earth, and trees;
True *sal-marinum* o' the seas;
The *farina* of beans an' pease,
        He has't in plenty;

Aqua-fontis, what you please,
$\qquad$ He can content ye.

22

'Forbye some new, uncommon weapons,
Urinus spiritus of capons;
Or mite-horn shavings, filings, scrapings,
$\qquad$ Distill'd *per se*;
Sal-alkali o' midge-tail-clippings,
$\qquad$ And moni mae.'

more

23

'Waes me for Johnie Ged's Hole now,'
Quoth I, 'if that thae news be true!
His braw calf-ward whare gowans grew
$\qquad$ Sae white and bonie,
Nae doubt they'll rive it wi' the plew:
$\qquad$ They'll ruin Johnie!'

these
grazing plot;
daisies

split

24

The creature grain'd an eldritch laugh
And says: 'Ye needna yoke the pleugh,
Kirkyards will soon be till'd eneugh,
$\qquad$ Tak ye name fear:
They'll a' be trench'd wi monie a sheugh
$\qquad$ In twa-three year.

groaned

ditch

25

'Whare I kill'd ane, a fair strae death
By loss o' blood or want o' breath,
This night I'm free to tak my aith,
$\qquad$ That Hornbook's skill

straw i.e. bed

cloth   Has clad a score i' their last claith
                By drap an' pill.

26

weaver   'An honest wabster to his trade,
fists   Whase wife's twa nieves were scarce well-bred,
aching   Gat tippence-worth to mend her head,
                When it was sair;
crept quietly   The wife slade cannie to her bed,
                But ne'er spak mair.

27

colic   'A countra laird had taen the batts,
commotion   Or some curmurring in his guts,
         His only son for Hornbook sets,
                An' pays him well:
pet-ewes   The lad, for twa guid gimmer-pets,
                Was laird himsel.

28

         'A bonie lass – ye kend her name –
swelled up; belly Some ill-blewn drink had hov'd her wame;
         She trusts hersel, to hid the shame,
                In Hornbook's care;
         Horn sent her aff to her lang hame
                To hide it there.

29

sample   'That's just a swatch o' Hornbook's way;
         Thus goes he on from day to day,
         Thus does he poison, kill, an' slay,
                An's weel paid for't;

Yet stops me o' my lawfu' prey
        Wi' his damn'd dirt:

30

'But, hark! I'll tell you of a plot,
Tho' dinna ye be speakin o't:
I'll nail the self-conceited sot,
        As dead's a herrin;
Niest time we meet, I'll wad a groat,   *next; wager*
        He gets his fairin!'   *reward*

31

But just as he began to tell,
The auld kirk-hammer strak the bell
Some wee short hour ayont the twal,   *small; beyond*
        Which raised us baith: *twelve*
         got us to our legs
I took the way that pleas'd mysel,
        And sae did Death.

<hr />

The Brigs of Ayr

A Poem

INSCRIBED TO JOHN BALLANTINE, ESQ., AYR

Sir, think not with a mercenary view
Some servile Sycophant approaches you.
To you my Muse would sing these simple lays,
To you my heart its grateful homage pays,

I feel the weight of all your kindness past,
But thank you not as wishing it to last;
Scorn'd be the wretch whose earth-born grov'lling
    soul
Would in his ledger-hopes in Friends enroll.
Tho' I, a lowly, nameless, rustic Bard,
Who ne'er must hope your goodness to reward,
Yet man to man, Sir, let us fairly meet,
And like masonic Level, equal greet.
How poor the balance! ev'n what Monarch's plan,
Between two noble creatures such as Man.
That to your Friendship I am strongly tied
I still shall own it, Sir, with grateful pride,
When haply roaring seas between us tumble wide.

Or if among so many cent'ries waste,
Thro the long vista of dark ages past,
Some much-lov'd honor'd name a radiance cast,
Perhaps some Patriot of distinguish'd worth,
I'll match him if My Lord will please step forth,
Or Gentleman and Citizen combine,
And I shall shew his peer in Ballantine:
Tho' honest men were parcell'd out for sale,
He might be shown a sample for the hale.

The simple Bard, rough at the rustic plough,
Learning his tuneful trade from ev'ry bough
(The chanting linnet, or the mellow thrush,
Hailing the setting sun, sweet, in the green thorn bush;
The soaring lark, the perching red-breast shrill,
Or deep-ton'd plovers grey, wild-whistling o'er the
    hill):

Shall he – nurst in the peasant's lowly shed,
To hardy independence bravely bred,
By early poverty to hardship steel'd,
And train'd to arms in stern misfortune's field –
Shall he be guilty of their hireling crimes,
The servile, mercenary Swiss of rhymes?
Or labour hard the panegyric close,
With all the venal soul of dedicating prose?
No! though his artless strains he rudely sings,
And throws his hand uncouthly o'er the stings,
He glows with all the spirit of the bard,
Fame, honest fame, his great, his dear reward.
Still, if some patron's gen'rous care he trace,
Skill'd in the secret to bestow with grace;
When Ballantine befriends his humble name,
And hands the rustic stranger up to fame,
With heartfelt throes his grateful bosom swells:
The godlike bliss, to give, alone excels.

'Twas when the stacks get on their winter hap,
And thack and rape secure the toil-won crap;   thatch; rope; crop
Potatoe-bings are snuggèd up frae skaith   heaps; damage
O' coming winter's biting, frosty breath;
The bees, rejoicing o'er their summer toils –
Unnumber'd buds' an' flowers' delicious spoils,
Seal'd up with frugal care in massive waxen piles –
Are doom'd by man, that tyrant o'er the weak,
The death o' devils smoor'd wi' brimstone reek: smothered;
                                                  smoke
The thundering guns are heard on ev'ry side,
The wounded coveys, reeling, scatter wide;
The feather'd field-mates, bound by Natures tie,

Sires, mother, children, in one carnage lie:
(What warm, poetic heart but inly bleeds,
And execrates man's savage, ruthless deeds!)
Nae mair the flower in field or meadow springs;
Nae mair the grove with airy concert rings,
Except perhaps the robin's whistling glee,
Proud o' the height o' some bit half-lang tree; small half-grown
The hoary morns precede the sunny days;
Mild, calm, serene, widespreads the noontide blaze,
While thick the gossamour waves wanton in the rays.

'Twas in that season, when a simple Bard,
Unknown and poor – simplicity's reward! –
Ae night, within the ancient brugh of Ayr, One
By whim inspir'd, or haply prest wi' care,
He left his bed, and took his wayward route,
And down by Simpson's wheel'd the left about
(Whether impell'd by all-directing Fate,
To witness what I after shall narrate;
Or whether, rapt in meditation high,
He wander'd forth, he knew not where nor why):
The drowsy Dungeon-Clock had number'd two,
And Wallace Tower had sworn the fact was true;
And tide-swoln Firth, with sullen-sounding roar,
Through the still night dash'd hoarse along the shore;
All else was hush'd as Nature's closèd e'e;
The silent moon shore high o'er tower and tree;
The chilly frost, beneath the silver beam,
Crept, gently-crusting, o'er the glittering stream.

When, lo! on either hand the list'ning Bard,
The clanging sugh of whistling wings is heard; swish

Two dusky forms dart thro' the midnight air,
Swift as the gos drives on the wheeling hare;
Ane on th' Auld brig his airy shape uprears,
The ither flutters o're the rising piers:
Our warlock rhymer instantly descried   wizard
The Sprites that owre the Brigs of Ayr preside.
(That bards are second-sighted is nae joke,
And ken the lingo of the sp'ritual folk;   know
Fays, spunkies, kelpies, a', they can explain them,   jack-o'-
                                                         lanthorns;
And ev'n the vera deils they brawly ken them.)   water-demons
Auld Brig appear'd of ancient Pictish race,   know them well
The vera wrinkles Gothic in his face;
He seem'd as he wi' Time had warstl'd lang,   wrestled
Yet, teughly doure, he bade an unco bang.   toughly stubborn
New Brig was buskit in a braw new coat,
That he, at Lon'on, frae ane Adams got;
In's hand five taper staves as smooth's a bead,
Wi' virls an' whirlygigums at the head.   rings; flourishes
The Goth was stalking round with anxious search,
Spying the time-worn flaws in ev'ry arch.
It chanc'd his new-come neebor took his e'e,
And e'en a vex'd and angry heart had he!   forbidding
Wi' thieveless sneer to see his modish mien,
He, down the water, gies him this guid-een:–   river

AULD BRIG

'I doubt na, frien', ye'll think ye're nae sheep-
    shank,
Ance ye were streekit owre frae bank to bank!   stretched across
But gin ye be a brig as auld as me –   when

Tho' faith, that date, I doubt, ye'll never see –
wager a
farthing
There'll be, if that day come, I'll wad a boddle,
crotchets
Some fewer whigmeleeries in your noddle.'

NEW BRIG

discretion
'Auld Vandal! ye but show your little mense,
Just much about it wi' your scanty sense:
Will your poor, narrow foot-path of a street,
Where twa wheel-barrows tremble when they meet,
Your ruin'd, formless bulk o' stane an' lime,
Compare wi' bonie brigs o' modern time?
There's men of taste would tak the Ducat stream,
Tho' they should cast the vera sark an swim,
E'er they would grate their feelings wi' the view
O' sic an ugly, Gothic hulk as you.'

AULD BRIG

cuckoo
'Conceited gowk! puff'd up wi' windy pride!
This monie a year I've stood the flood an' tide;
eld; worn out
And tho' wi' crazy eild I'm sair forfairn,
pile of stones
I'll be a brig when ye're a shapeless cairn!
As yet ye little ken about the matter,
But twa-three winters will inform ye better.
When heavy, dark, continued, a'-day rains
Wi' deepening deluges o'erflow the plains;
When from the hills where springs the brawling Coil,
Or stately Lugar's mossy fountains boil,
Or where the Greenock winds his moorland course,
Or haunted Garpal draws his feeble source,

Arous'd by blustering winds an' spotting thowes,   *thaws*
In monie a torrent down the snaw-broo rowes;   *snow-brew rolls*
While crashing ice, borne on the roaring speat,   *flood*
Sweeps dams, an' mills, an' brigs, a' to the gate;   *the road*
And from Glenbuck down to the Ratton-Key
Auld Ayr is just one lengthen'd, tumbling sea –   *seaward*
Then down ye'll hurl (deil nor ye never rise!),   *crash*
And dash the gumlie jaups up to the pouring skies!   *muddy splashes*
A lesson sadly teaching, to your cost,
That Architecture's noble art is lost!'

NEW BRIG

  'Fine architecture, trowth, I needs must say't o't,
The Lord be thankit that we've tint the gate o't!   *lost the trick*
Gaunt, ghastly, ghaist-alluring edifices,
Hanging with threat'ning jut, like precipices;
O'er-arching, mouldy, gloom-inspiring coves,
Supporting roofs fantastic – stony groves;
Windows and doors in nameless sculptures drest,
With order, symmetry, or taste unblest;
Forms like some bedlam statuary's dream,
The craz'd creations of misguided whim;
Forms might be worshipp'd on the bended knee,
And still the second dread Command be free:
Their likeness is not found on earth, in air, or sea!
Mansions that would disgrace the building taste
Of any mason reptile, bird or beast,
Fit only for a doited monkish race,   *muddled*
Or frosty maids forsworn the dear embrace,
Or cuifs of later times, wha held the notion,   *dolts*

That sullen gloom was sterling true devotion:
Fancies that our guid brugh denies protection,
And soon may they expire, unblest with resurrection!'

AULD BRIG

'O ye, my dear-remember'd, ancient yearlings, — coevals
Were ye but here to share my wounded feelings!
Ye worthy proveses, an' monie a bailie, — provosts
Wha in the paths o' righteousness did toil ay;
Ye dainty deacons, an' ye douce conveeners; — sedate
To whom our moderns are but causey-cleaners; — causeway-
Ye godly councils, wha hae blest this town;
Ye godly brethren o' the sacred gown,
Wha meekly gie your hurdies to the smiters; — buttocks
And (what would now be strange), ye godly Writers;
A'ye douce folk I've borne aboon the broo, — sedate;
Were ye but here, what would ye say or do! — across; water
How would your spirits groan in deep vexation
To see each melancholy alteration;
And, agonising, curse the time and place
When ye begat the base degen'rate race!
Nae langer rêv'rend men, their country's glory,
In plain braid Scots hold forth a plain, braid story;
Nae langer thrifty citizens, an' douce,
Meet owre a pint or in the council-house;
But staumrel, corky-headed, gracelss gentry, — half-witted
The herryment and ruin of the country: — spoliation
Men three-parts made by tailors and by barbers,
Wha waste your weel-hain'd gear on damn'd New — well-saved
    Brigs and harbours!' — wealth

NEW BRIG

Now haud you there! for faith ye've said enough,
And muckle mair than ye can mak to through. make good
As for your priesthood, I shall say but little,
Corbies and clergy are a shot right kittle: ravens; sort; ticklish
But, under favour o' your langer beard,
Abuse o' magistrates might weel be spar'd;
To liken them to your auld-warld squad,
I must needs say, comparisons are odd.
In Ayr, wag-wits nae mair can hae a handle
To mouth 'a Citizen,' a term o' scandal;
Nae mair the council waddles down the street,
In all the pomp of ignorant conceit;
Men wha grew wise priggin owre hops an' raisins, haggling
Or gather'd lib'ral views in bonds and seisins;
If haply Knowledge, on a random tramp,
Had shor'd them with a glimmer of his lamp, menaced
And would to common-sense for once betray'd them,
Plain, dull stupidity stept kindly in to aid them.'

What farther clish-ma-claver might been said, nonsense
What bloody wars, if Sprites had blood to shed,
No man can tell; but, all before their sight,
A fairy train appear'd in order bright:
Adown the glittering stream they featly danc'd;
Bright to the moon their various dresses glanc'd;
They footed o'er the wat'ry glass so neat,
The infant ice scarce bent beneath their feet;
While arts of minstrelsy among them rung,
And soul-ennobling Bards heroic ditties sung.

(cat-) gut-

O, had M'Lauchlan, thairm-inspiring sage,
Been there to hear this heavenly band engage,
When thro' his dear strathspeys they bore with
    Highland rage;
Or when they struck old Scotia's melting airs,
The lover's raptured joys or bleeding cares;

ear

How would his Highland lug been nobler fir'd,
And ev'n his matchless hand with finer touch
    inspir'd!
No guess could tell what instrument appear'd,
But all the soul of Music's self was heard;
Harmonious concert rung in every part,
While simply melody pour'd moving on the heart.

The Genius of the Stream in front appears,
A venerable chief advanc'd in years;
His hoary head with water-lilies crown'd,
His manly leg with garter-tangle bound.
Next came the loveliest pair in all the ring,
Sweet Female Beauty hand in hand with Spring;
Then, crown'd with flow'ry hay, came Rural Joy,
And Summer, with his fervid-beaming eye:
All-cheering Plenty, with her flowing horn,
Led yellow Autumn wreath'd with nodding corn;
Then Winter's time-bleach'd locks did hoary show,
By Hospitality, with cloudless brow.
Next follow'd Courage, with his martial stride,
From where the Feal wild-woody coverts hide;
Benevolence, with mild, benignant air,
A female form, came from the towers of Stair;
Learning and Worth in equal measures trode

From simple Catrine, their long-lov'd abode;
Last, white-rob'd Peace, crown'd with a hazel wreath,
To rustic Agriculture did bequeath
The broken, iron instruments of death:
At sight of whom our Sprites forgat their kindling wrath.

<hr />

Address To The Unco Guid

ON THE RIGIDLY RIGHTEOUS

My Son, these maxims make a rule,
  An' lump them ay thegither:
The Rigid Righteous is a fool,
  The Rigid Wise anither;
The cleanest corn that e'er was dight   sifted
  May hae some pyles o' caff in;   chaff
So ne'er a fellow-creature slight
  For random fits o' daffin   larking
                    Solomon (Eccles. vii. 16)

1

O ye, wha are sae guid yoursel,
  Sae pious and sae holy,
Ye've nought to do but mark and tell
  Your neebours' fauts and folly;
Whase life is like a weel-gaun mill,   well-going
  Supplied wi' store o' water;

hopper
clapper

The heapet happer's ebbing still,
 An' still the clap plays clatter!

2

company

Hear me, ye venerable core,
 As counsel for poor mortals

sober
giddy

That frequent pass douce Wisdom'd door
 For glaikit Folly's portals:

put forward

I for their thoughtless, careless sakes
 Would here propone defences –

restive

Their donsie tricks, their black mistakes,
 Their failings and mischances.

3

Ye see your state wi' theirs compared,
 And shudder at the niffer;

exchange

But cast a moment's fair regard,
 What makes the mighty differ?
Discount what scant occasion gave;
 That purity ye pride in;

rest

And (what's aft mair than a' the lave)
 Your better art o' hidin.

4

Think, when your castigated pulse
 Gies now and then a wallop,
What ragings must his veins convulse,
 That still eternal gallop!
Wi' wind and tide fair i' your tail,
 Right on ye scud your sea-way;
But in the teeth o' baith to sail,

uncommon

 It maks an unco lee-way

131

5

See Social-life and Glee sit down
   All joyous and unthinking,
Till, quite transmugrify'd, they're grown
   Debauchery and Drinking:
O, would they stay to calculate,
   Th' eternal consequences,
Or – your more dreaded hell to state –
   Damnation of expenses!

6

Ye high, exalted, virtuous dames,
   Tied up in godly laces,
Before ye gie poor Frailty names,
   Suppose a change o' cases:
A dear-lov'd lad, convenience snug,
   A treach'rous inclination –
But, let me whisper i' your lug,   ear
   Ye're aiblins nae temptation.   maybe

7

Then gently scan your brother man,
   Still gentler sister woman;
Tho' they may gang a kennin wrang,
To step aside is human:
   One point must still be greatly dark,
The moving *why* they do it;
   And just as lamely can ye mark
How far perhaps they rue it.

8

Who make the heart, 'tis He alone
    Decidedly can try us:
He knows each chord, its various tone,
    Each spring, its various bias:
Then at the balance let's be mute,
    We never can adjust it;
What's done we partly may compute,
    But know not what's resisted.

<hr />

Tam Samson's Elegy

An honest man's the noblest work of God.

POPE

1

Has auld Kilmarnock seen the Deil?
Or great Mackinlay thrawn his heel?
Or Robertson again grown weel
       To preach an' read?
worse; everybody 'Na, waur than a'!' cries ilka chiel,
       'Tam Samson's dead!'

2

groan Kilmarnock lang may grunt an' grane,
weep alone An' sigh, an' sab, an' greet her lane,
clothe; child An' cleed her bairns – man, wife an' wean –
       In mourning weed;
rent in kind To Death she's dearly pay'd the kain:
       Tam Samson's dead!

133

3

The Brethren o' the mystic level   slope
May hing their head in woefu' bevel,
While by their nose the tears will revel,
      Like onie bead;
Death's gien the Lodge an unco devel: stunning blow
      Tam Samson's dead!

4

When Winter muffles up his cloak,
And binds the mire like a rock;
When to the loughs the curlers flock,   ponds
      Wi' gleesome speed,
Wha will they station at the cock?   mark
      Tam Samson's dead!

5

He was the king of a' the core   company
To guard, or draw, or wick a bore,
Or up the rink like Jehu roar
      In time o' need;
but now he lags on Death's hog-score:
      Tam Samson's dead!

6

Now safe the stately sawmont sail,   salmon
And trouts bedropp'd wi' crimson hail,
And eels, weel-kend for souple tail,
      And geds for greed,   pikes
Since, dark in Death's fish-creel, we wail,
      Tam Samson dead!

7

partridges
leg-plumed;
confidently
hares; tail

Rejoice, ye birring paitricks a';
Ye cootie moorcocks, crousely craw;
Ye maukins, cock your fud fu' braw
    Withouten dread;
Your mortal fae is now awa:
    Tam Samson's dead!

8

attire

That woefu' morn be ever mourn'd,
Saw him in shootin graith adorn'd,
While pointers round impatient burn'd,
    Frae couples free'd;
But och! he gaed and ne'er ruturn'd:
    Tam Samson's dead.

9

ankles
brooks; lakes

weeping

In vain auld-age his body batters,
In vain the gout his ancles fetters,
In vain the burns can down like waters,
    An acre braid!
Now ev'ry auld wife, greetin, clatters:
    'Tam Samson's dead!'

10

bog

feud
blast

Owre monie a weary hag he limpit,
An' ay the tither shot he thumpit,
Till coward Death behind him jumpit,
    Wi' deadly feide;
Now he proclaims wi' tout o' trumpet:
    'Tam Samson's dead!'

11

When at his heart he felt the dagger,
He reel'd his wonted bottle-swagger,
But yet he drew the mortal trigger
  Wi' weel-aim'd heed;
'Lord, five!' he cry'd, an' owre did stagger –
  Tam Samson's dead!

12

Ilk hoary hunter mourn'd a brither; Each
Ilk sportsman-youth bemoan'd a father;
Yon auld gray stane, amang the heather,
  Marks out his head;
Whare Burns has wrote, in rhyming blether: babble
  'Tam Samson's dead!'

13

There low he lies in lasting rest;
Perhaps upon his mould'ring breast
Some spitefu' moorfowl bigs her nest, builds
  To hatch an' breed:
Alas! nae mair he'll them molest:
  Tam Samson's dead!

14

When August winds the heather wave,
And sportsmen wander by yon grave,
Three volleys let his memory crave
  O' pouther an' lead,
Till Echo answers frae her cave:
  'Tam Samson's dead!'

15

'Heav'n rest his saul whare'er he be!'
more   Is th' wish o' monie mae than me:
He has twa fauts, or maybe three,
          Yet what remead?
One   Ae social, honest man want we:
          Tam Samson's dead!

THE EPITAPH

Tam Samson's weel-worn clay here lies:
    Ye canting zealots, spare him!
If honest worth in Heaven rise,
    Ye'll mend or ye win near him.

PER CONTRA

Go, Fame, an' canter like a filly
Thro' a' the streets an neuks o' Killie'
fellow   Tell ev'ry social honest billie
          To cease his grievin;
quick knife   For, yet unskaith'd by Death's gleg gullie,
          Tam Samson's leevin!

Address to a Haggis

1

Fair fa' your honest, sonsie face,　　　　　　　*jolly*
Great chieftain o' the puddin-race!
Aboon them a' ye tak your place,　　　　　　　*Above*
　　　　　　Painch, tripe, or thairm:　　　*Paunch;*
Weel are ye wordy of a grace　　　　　　　　*small guts*
　　　　　　As lang's my arm.

2

The groaning trencher there ye fill,
Your hurdies like a distant hill,　　　　　　　*buttocks*
Your pin wad help to mend a mill　　　　　　　*skewer*
　　　　　　In time o' need,
While thro' your pores the dews distil
　　　　　　Like amber bead.

3

His knife see rustic Labour dight,　　　　　　　*wipe*
An' cut ye up wi' ready slight,　　　　　　　*skill*
Trenching your gushing entrails bright,
　　　　　　Like onie ditch;
And then, O what a glorious sight,
　　　　　　Warm-reekin, rich!

4

Then, horn for horn, they stretch an' strive:　　　*spoon*
Deil tak the hindmost, on they drive,
Till a' their weel-swall'd kytes belyve　　*bellies; by-and-bye*
　　　　　　Are bent like drums;
Then auld Guidman, maist like to rive,　　　　　*burst*
　　　　　　'Bethankit!' hums.

138

5

Is ther that owre his French *ragout,*
Or *olio* that wad staw a sow,
Or *fricassee* wad mak her spew
   Wi' perfect sconner,
Looks down wi' sneering, scornfu' view
   On sic a dinner?

sicken

disgust

6

Poor devil! see him owre his trash,
As feckless as a wither'd rash,
His spindle shank a guid whip-lash,
   His nieve a nit;
Thro' bluidy flood or field to dash,
   O how unfit!

weak; rush

fist; nut

7

But mark the Rustic, haggis-fed,
The trembling earth resounds his tread,
Clap in his walie nieve a blade,
   He'll make it whissle;
An' legs, an' arms, an' heads will sned
   Like taps o' thrissle.

ample

crop

8

Ye Pow'rs, wha mak mankind your care,
And dish them out their bill o' fare,
Auld Scotland wants nae skinking ware,
   That jaups in luggies;
But, if ye wish her gratfu' prayer,
   Gie her a Haggis!

watery

splashes;
porringers

Elegy on Captain Matthew Henderson

A GENTLEMAN WHO HELD THE PATENT FOR HIS HONOURS IMMEDIATELY FROM ALMIGHTY GOD

But now his radiant course is run,
For Matthew's course was bright:
His soul was like the glorious sun
A matchless, Heavenly light.

1

O Death! thou tyrant fell and bloody!
The meikle Devil wi' a woodie   great; halter
Haurl thee hame to his black smiddie   Trail; smithy
      O'er hurcheon hides,   hedgehog
And like stock-fish come o'er his studdie   anvil
      Wi' thy auld sides!

2

He's gane, he's gane! he's frae us torn,   gone
The ae best fellow e'er was born!   one
Thee, Matthew, Nature's s sel shall mourn,
      By wood and wild,
Where, haply, Pity, strays forlorn,
      Frae man exil'd.

3

stars   Ye hills, near neebors o' the starns,
mounds   That proudly cock your cresting cairns!
      Ye cliffs, the haunts of sailing yearns,
           Where Echo slumbers!
      Come join ye, nature's sturdiest bairns.
           My wailing numbers!

4

every   Mourn, ilka grove the cushat kens!
woods   Ye hazly shaws and briery dens!
brooklets, winding Ye burnies, wimplin down your glens
purling   Wi' toddlin din,
quick leaps   Or foaming, strang, wi' hasty stens,
fall   Frae lin to lin!

5

      Mourn, little harebells o'er the lea;
      Ye stately foxgloves, fair to see;
      Ye woodbines, hanging bonilie
           In scented bowers;
      Ye roses on your thorny tree,
           The first o'flowers!

6

      At dawn, when every grassy blade
      Droops with a diamond at this head;
      At ev'n, when beans their fragrance shed
           I' th' rustling gale;
hares, scudding Ye maukins, whiddin through the glade;
           Come join my wail!

7

Mourn, ye wee songsters o' the wood;
Ye grouse that crap the heather bud;
Ye curlews, calling thro' a clud;   cloud
        Ye whistling plover;
And mourn, ye whirring paitrick brood: partidge
        He's gane for ever!

8

Mourn, sooty coots, and speckled teals;
Ye fisher herons, watching eels;
Ye duck and drake, wi' airy wheels
        Circling the lake;
Ye bitterns, till the quagmire reels,
        Rair for his sake!   Boom

9

Mourn, clam'ring craiks, at close o' day,   corncrakes
'Mang field o' flow'ring clover gay!
And when you wing your annual way
        Frae our cauld shore,
Tell thae far warlds wha lies in clay,   those
        Wham we deplore.

10

Ye houlets, frae your ivy bower   owls
In some auld tree, or eldritch tower,   haunted
What time the moon, wi' silent glowr,   stare
        Sets up her horn,
Wail thro' the dreary midnight hour
        Till waukrife morn!   wakeful

11

O rivers, forest, hills, and plains!

cheerful

Oft have ye heard my canty strains:
But now, what else for me remains
          But tales of woe?

eyes
Must

And frae my een the drapping rains
          Maun ever flow.

12

Mourn, Spring, thou darling of the year!

catch

Ilk cowslip cup shall kep a tear:
Thou, Simmer, while each corny spear
          Shoots up its head,
Thy gay, green, flowery tresses shear
          For him that's dead!

13

Thou, Autumn, wi' thy yellow hair,
In grief thy sallow mantle tear!
Thou, Winter, hurling thro' the air
          The roaring blast,
Wide o'er the naked world declare
          The worth we've lost!

14

Mourn him, thou Sun, great source of light!
Mourn, Empress of the silent night!

starlets

And you, ye twinkling starnies birght,
          My Matthew mourn!
For through your orbs he's taen his flight,
          Ne'er to return.

15

O Henderson! the man! the brother!
And art thou gone, and gone for ever?
And hast thou crost that unknown river,
   Life's dreary bound?
Like thee, where shall I find another,
   The world around?

16

Go to your sculptur'd tombs, ye Great,
In a' the tinsel trash o' state!
But by thy honest turf I'll wait,
   Thou man of worth!
And weep the ae best fellow's fate
   E'er lay in earth!

THE EPITAPH

1

Stop, passenger! my story's brief,
 And truth I shall relate, man:
I tell nae common tale o' grief,
 For Matthew was a great man.

2

If thou uncommon merit hast,
 Yet spurn'd at Fortune's door, man;
A look of pity hither cast,
 For Matthew was a poor man,

3

If thou a noble sodger art,

That passest by this grave, man;
There moulders here a gallant heart,
    For Matthew was a brave man.

4

If thou on men, their works and ways,
    Canst throw uncommon light, man;
Here lies wha weel had won thy praise,
    For Matthew was a bright man.

5

If thou, at Friendship's sacred ca'.
    Wad life itself resign, man;
Thy sympathetic tear maun fa',
    For Matthew was a kind man.

6

If thou art staunch, without a stain,
    Like the unchanging blue, man;
This was a kinsman o' thy ain,
    For Matthew was a true man.

7

If thou hast wit, and fun, and fire,
    And ne'er guid wind did fear, man;
brother   This was thy billie, dam, and sire,
    For Matthew was a queer man.

8

whining   If onie whiggish, whigin sot,
    To blame poor Matthew dare, man;
woe   May dool and sorrow be his lot!
    For Matthew was a rare man.

Tam o' Shanter

A Tale

Of Brownyis and of Bogillis full is this Buke
GAWIN DOUGLAS

When chapman billies leave the street,	pedlar fellows
And drouthy neebors neebors meet;	thirsty
As market-days are wearing late,	
An' folk begin to tak the gate;	road
While we sit bousing at the nappy,	ale
An' getting fou and unco happy,	full; mighty
We think na on the lang Scots miles,	not
The mosses, waters, slaps, and styles,	bogs; pools; breaches; stiles
That lie between us and our hame,	
Whare sits our sulky, sullen dame,	
Gathering her brows like gathering storm,	
Nursing her wrath to keep it warm.	

This truth fand honest Tam o' Shanter,	found
As he frae Ayr ae night did canter:	one
(Auld Ayr, wham ne'er a town surpasses.	
For honest men and bonie lasses.)	

O Tam, had'st thou but sae wise,	
As taen thy ain wife Kate's advice!	to have taken
She tauld thee weel thou was a skellum,	good-for-nothing
A blethering, blustering, drunken blellum;	chattering; babbler
That frae November till October,	
Ae market-day thou was nae sober;	
That ilka melder wi' the miller,	meal-grinding

146

money
shod

Thou sat as lang as thou had siller;
That ev'ry naig was ca'd a shoe on,
The smith and thee gat roaring fou on;
That at the Lord's house, even on Sunday,
Thou drank wi' Kirkton Jean till Monday.
She prophesied, that, late or soon,
Thou would be found deep drown'd in Doon,

wizards;
dark

Or catch'd wi' warlocks in the mirk
By Alloway's auld, haunted kirk.

makes; weep

Ah! gentle dames, it gars me greet,
To think how monie counsels sweet,
How monie lengthen'd, sage advices
The husband frae the wife despises!

But to our tale:- Ae market-night,

uncommonly

Tam had got planted unco right,
Fast by an ingle, bleezing finely,

foaming new
ale
Cobbler

Wi' reaming swats, that drank divinely;
And as his elbow, Souter Johnie,
His ancient, trusty, drouthy cronie:
Tam lo'ed him like a very brither;
They had been fou for weeks thegither.
The night drave on wi' sangs and clatter;
And ay the ale was growing better:
The landlady and Tam grew gracious:
Wi' secret favours, sweet and precious:
The Souter tauld his queerest stories;
The landlord's laugh was ready chorus;

roar

The storm without might rair and rustle,
Tam did na mind the storm a whistle.

Care, mad to see a man sae happy,
E'en drown'd himsel amang the nappy.
As bees flee hame wi' lades o' treasure,
The minutes wing'd their way wi' pleasure:
Kings may be blest but Tam was glorious,
O'er a' the ills o' life victorious!

But pleasures are like poppies spread:
You seize the flow'r, its bloom is shed;
Or like the snow falls in the river,
A moment white – then melts for ever;
Or like the Borealis race,
That flit ere you can point their place;
Or like the rainbow's lovely form
Evanishing amid the storm.
Nae man can tether time or tide;
The hour approaches Tam maun ride: must
That hour, o' night's black arch the key-stane,
That dreary hour Tam mounts his beast in;
An sic a night he taks the road in,
As ne'er poor sinner was abroad in.

The wind blew as 'twad blawn its last;   would have
The rattling showers rose on the blast;
The speedy gleams the darkness swallow'd;
Loud, deep, and lang the thunder bellow'd;
That night, a child might understand,
The Deil had business on his hand.

Weel mounted on his grey meare Meg,
A better never lifted leg,

spanked;puddle	Tam skelpit on thro' dub and mire,
	Despising wind, and rain, and fire;
Now	Whiles holding fast his guid blue bonnet,
song	Whiles crooning o'er some auld Scots sonnet,
staring	Whiles glow'ring round wi' prudent cares,
hobgoblins	Lest bogles catch him unawares:
	Kirk-Alloway was drawing nigh,
owls	Whare ghaists and houlets nightly cry.

across	By this time he was cross the ford,
smothered	Whare in the snaw the chapman smoor'd;
briches; big	And past the birks and meikle stane,
	Whare drunken charlie brak's nech-bane;
furze; pile of stones	And thro' the whins, and by the cairn,
	Whare hunters fand the murder'd bairn;
above	And near the thorn, aboon the well,
	Whare Mungo's mither hang'd hersel.
	Before him Doon pours all his floods;
	the doubling storm roars thro' the woods;
	The lightnings flash from pole to pole;
	Near and more near the thunders roll:
	When, glimmering thro' the groaning trees,
	Kirk-Alloway seem'd in a bleeze,
very chink	Thro' ilka bore the beams were glancing,
	And loud resounded mirth and dancing.

	Inspiring, bold John Barleycorn!
	What dangers thou canst make us scorn!
ale	Wi' tippenny, we fear nae evil;
whisky	Wi' usquabae, we'll face the Devil!
	The swats sae ream'd in Tammie's noddle,

Fair play, he car'd na deils a boddle.
But Maggie stood, right sair astonish'd,
Till, by the heel and hand admonish'd,
She ventur'd forward on the light;
And wow! Tam saw an unco sight!   *wondrous*

 Warlocks and witches in a dance;
Nae cotillion, brent new fraw France,   *brand*
But hornpipes, jigs, strathspeys, and reels
Put life and mettle in their heels.
A winnock-bunker in the east,   *window-seat*
There sat auld Nick, in shape o' beast;
A tousie tyke, black, grim, and large,   *shaggy dog*
To gie them music was his charge:
He screw's the pipes and gart them skirl,   *squeal*
Till roof and rafters a' did dirl.   *ring*
Coffins stood round, like open presses,   *cupboards*
That shaw'd the dead in their last dresses;
And, by some devilish cantraip sleight,   *magic device*
Each in its cauld hand held a light:
By which heroic Tam was able
To note upon the haly table,
A murderer's banes, in gibbet-airns;   *-irons*
Twa span-lang, wee, unchristen'd bairns;
A thief new-cutted frae a rape –
Wi' his last gasp his gab did gape;   *mouth*
Five tomahwks wi' bluid red-rusted;
Five scymitars wi' murder crusted;
A garter which a babe had strangled;
A knife a father's throat had mangled –
Whom his ain son o' life bereft –

The grey-hairs yet stack to the heft;
Wi' mair of horrible and awefu'.
Which even to name wad be unlawfu'.
Three Lawyers' tongues, turned inside out,
Wi' lies seamed like a beggar's clout;
Three Priests' hearts, rotten, black as muck,
Lay stinking, vile, in every neuk.

stared   As Tammie glowr'd, amaz'd, and curious,
The mirth and fun grew fast and furious;
The piper loud and louder blew,
The dancers quick and quicker flew,
took hold   They reel'd, they set, they cross'd, they cleekit,
every hag
sweated   Till ilka carlin swat and reekit,
rags   And coost her duddies to the wark,
tripped   And linket at it in her sark!

these   Now Tam, O Tam! had thae been queans,
A' plump and strapping in their teens!
greasy   Their sarks, instead o' creeshie flannen
Been naw-white seventeen hunder linen! –
These   Thir breeks o'mine, my only pair,
That ance were plush o' guid blue hair,
buttocks   I wad hae gi'en them off my hurdies
maidens   For ae blink o' the bonie burdies!

wizened   But wither'd beldams, auld and droll,
wean   Rigwoodie hags was spean a foa,
leaping;   Louping and flinging on a crummock,
kicking; cudgel
I wonder did na turn thy stomach!

well   But Tam kend what was what fu' brawlie:
comely; choice   There was ae winsome wench and wawlie,

151

That night enlisted in the core,   *company*
Lang after kend on Carrick shore
(For monie a beast to dead she shot,   *death*
An' perish'd monie a bonie boat,
And shook baith meikle corn and bear,   *much; barley*
And kept the country-side in fear.)
Her cutty sark, o' Paisley harn,   *short shift; coarse cloth*
That while a lassie she had worn,
In longitude tho' sorely scanty,
It was her best, and she was vauntie   *proud*
Ah! little kend thy reverend grannie,
That sark she coft for her wee Nannie,   *bought*
Wi' twa pund Scots ('twas a' her riches),
Wad ever grac'd a dance of witches!   *Would have*

But here my Muse her wing maun cour,   *stoop*
Sic flights as far beyond her power:
To sing how Nannie lap and flang   *leaped and kicked*
(A souple jad she was and strang);
And how Tam stood like ane bewitch'd,
And thought his very een enrich'd;
Even Satan glowr'd, and fidg'd fu' fain,   *fidgeted; fond*
And hotch'd and blew wi' might and main;   *jerked*
Till first ae caper, syne anither,   *then*
Tam tint his reason a' thegither,   *lost*
And roars out: 'Weel done, Cutty-sark!'
And in an instant all was dark;
And scarcely had he Maggie rallied,
When out the hellish legion sallied.

As bees bizz out wi' angry fyke,   *fret*
When plundering herds assail their byke;   *hive*

the hare's   As open pussie's mortal foes,
When pop! she starts before their nose;
As eager runs the market-crowd,
When 'Catch the thief!' resounds aloud:
So Maggie runs, the witches follow,

unearthly   Wi' monie an eldritch skriech and hollo.

Ah, Tam! Ah, Tam! thou'll get thy fairin!
In hell they'll roast thee like a herrin!
In vain thy Kate awaits thy comin!
Kate soon will be a woefu' woman!
Now, do thy speedy utmost, Meg,
And win the key-stane of the brig;
There, at them thou thy tail may toss,
A running stream they dare na cross!
But ere the key-stane she could make,

devil   The fient a tail she had to shake;
For Nannie, far before the rest,
Hard upon noble Maggie prest,

aim   And flew at Tam wi' furious ettle;
But little wist she Maggie's mettle!

whole   Ae spring brought off her master hale,
But left behind her ain grey tail:

seized   The carlin claught her by the rump,
And left poor Maggie scarce a stump.

No, wha this tale o' truth shall read,
Ilk man, and mother's son, take heed:
Whene'er to drink you are inclin'd,
Or cutty sarks run in your mind,
Think! ye may buy the joys o'er dear:
Remember Tam o' Shanter's meare.

153

Holy Willie's Prayer

And send the godly in a pet to pray

POPE

1

O Thou that in the Heavens does dwell,
Wha, as it pleases best Thysel,
Sends ane to Heaven an' ten to Hell
    A' for Thy glory,
And no for onie guid or ill
    They've done before Thee!

2

I bless and praise Thy matchless might,
When thousands Thou hast left in night,
That I am here before Thy sight,
    For gifts an' grace
A burning and a shining light
    To a' this place.

3

What was I, or my generation,
That I should get sic exaltation?   *such*
I, wha deserv'd most just damnation
    For broken laws
Sax thousand years ere my creation,   *Six*
    Thro Adam's cause!

4

When from my mither's womb I fell,
Thou might hae plung'd me deep in hell

gums

To gnash my gooms, and weep, and wail
    In burning lakes,
Whare damnèd devils roar and yell,
        Chain'd to their stakes.

5

Yet I am here, a chosen sample,
To show Thy grace is great and ample:
I'm here a pillar o' Thy temple,
        Strong as a rock,
A guide, a buckler, and example
        To a' Thy flock!

6

But yet, O Lord! confess I must:

irked

At times I'm fash'd wi' fleshly lust;
An' sometimes, too, in warldly trust,
        Vile self gets in;
But Thou remembers we are dust,
        Defiled wi' sin.

7

last night;
knowest

O Lord! yestreen, Thou kens, wi' Meg –
Thy pardon I sincerely beg –
O, may't ne'er be a living plague
        To my dishonour!
An' I'll ne'er lift a lawless leg
        Again upon her.

8

must

Besides, I farther maun avow –
Wi' Leezie's lass, three times, I trow –

But Lord, that Friday I was fou,   drunk
        When I cam near her,
Or else, Thou kens, Thy servant true
        Wad never steer her.   would;
        meddle with

9

Maybe Thou lets this fleshly thorn
Buffet Thy servant e'en and morn,
Lest he owre proud and high should turn
        That he's sae gifted: too
If sae, Thy han' maun e'en be borne
        Until Thou lift it.

10

Lord, bless Thy chosen in this place,
For here Thou has a chosen race!
But God confound their stubborn face
        An' blast their name,
Wha bring Thy elders to disgrace
        An' open shame!

11

Lord, mind Gau'n Hamilton's deserts
He drinks, an' swears, an' plays at cartes,   cards
Yet has sae monie takin arts
        Wi' great and sma',
Frae God's ain Priest the people's hearts
        He steals awa.

12

And when we chasten'd him therefore,
Thou kens how he bred sic a splore,   row

and set the warld in a road
O' laughin at us:
Curse Thou his basket and his store,
Kail an' potatoes!

13

Lord, hear my earnest cry and pray'r
Against that Presbyt'ry of Ayr!
Thy stong right hand, Lord mak it bare
Upo' their heads!
Lord, visit them, an dinna spare,
For their misdeeds!

do not

14

O Lord, my God!, that glib-tongu'd Aiken,
My vera heart and flesh are quakin
To think how we stood sweatin, shakin,
An' pish'd wi' dread,
While he, wi' hingin lip an' sankin,
Held up his head.

sneering

15

Lord, in Thy day o' vengeance try him!
Lord, visit him wha did employ him!
And pass not in Thy mercy by them,
Nor hear their pray'r,
But for Thy people's sake destroy them,
An dinna spare!

16

But Lord, remember me and mine
Wi' mercies temporal and divine,

That I for grace an' gear may shine   *wealth*
           Excell'd by name;
And a' the glory shall be Thine –
           Amen, Amen!

<hr />

Address of Beelzebub

To the Right Honorable the Earl of
Breadalbane, President of the Right Honorable the
Highland Society, which met on the 23rd of May
last, at the Shakespeare, Covent Garden, to
concert ways and means to frustrate the designs of
five hundred Highlanders who, as the Society were
informed by Mr. M'Kenzie of Applecross, were so
audacious as to attempt an escape from their
lawful lords and masters whose property they
were, by emigrating from the lands of Mr.
Macdonald of Glengary to the wilds of Canada, in
search of that fantastic thing – Liberty.

Long life, my lord, an' health be yours,
Unskaith'd by hunger'd Highland boors!   *Unharmed*
Lord grant nae duddie, desperate beggar,   *ragged*
Wi' dirk, claymore, or rusty trigger,
May twin auld Scotland o' a life   *rob*
She likes – as lambkins like a knife!

Faith! you and Applecross were right
To keep the Highland hounds in sight!
offer I doubt na! they wad bid nae better
Than let them ance out owre the water!
those Then up amang thae lakes and seas,
They'll mak what rules and laws they please:
Some daring Hancock, or a Franklin,
May set their Highland bluid a-ranklin;
Some Washington again may head them,
Or some Montgomerie, fearless, lead them;

Till (God knows what may be effected
When by such heads and hearts directed)
Poor dunghill sons of dirt an' mire
May to Patrician rights aspire!
Nae sage North now, nor sager Sackville,
To watch and premier owre the pack vile!
An' whare will ye get Howes and Clintons
To bring them to a right repentance?
scare To cowe the rebel generation,
An' save the honor o' the nation?
They, an' be damn'd! what right hae they
To meat or sleep or light o' day,
Far less to riches, pow'r, or freedom,
But what your lordship likes to gie them?

But hear, my lord! Glengary, hear!
too Your hand's owre light on them, I fear:
Your factors, grieves, trustees, and bailies,
gaily I canna say but they do gaylies:
They lay aside a' tender mercies,

An' tirl the hullions to the birses.   *strip; slovens; bristles*
Yet while they're only poind and herriet,   *distrained; robbed*
They'll keep their stubborn Highland spirit.
But smash them! crush them a' to spails,
An' rot the dyvors i' the jails!   *bankrupts*
The young dogs, swinge them to the labour:
Let wark an' hunger mak them sober!
The hizzies, if they're aughtlins fawsont,   *girls; at all good-looking*
Let them in Drury Lane be lesson'd!
An' if the wives an' dirty brats
Come thiggin at your doors an' yetts,   *begging; gates*
Flaffin wi' duds an' grey wi' beas',   *flapping with rags; vermin*
Frightin awa your deuks an' geese,   *ducks*
Get out a horsewhip or a jowler,   *bull dog*
The langest thong, the fiercest growler,
An' gar the tatter'd gypsies pack   *make*
Wi' a' their bastards on their back!

Go on, my Lord! I lang to meet you,   *long*
An' in my 'house at hame' to greet you.
Wi' common lords ye shanna mingle: *shall not*
The benmost neuk beside the ingle,   *inmost corner; fireside*
At my right han' assigned your seat
'Tween Herod's hip an' Polycrate,
Or (if you on your station tarrow)   *weary*
Between Almagro and Pizarro,
A seat, I'm sure ye're weel deservin't;
An' till ye come – your humble servant,

                         BEELZEBUB

Hell,
1st June, Anno Mundi 5790

The Tree of Liberty

1

Heard ye o' the Tree o' France,
    And wat ye what's the name o't?
Around it a' the patriots dance –
    Weel Europe kens the fame o't!
It stands where ance the Bastile stood –
    A prison built by kings, man,
When Superstition's hellish brood
    Kept France in leading-strings, man.

wot

2

Upo' this tree there grows sic fruit,
    Its virtues a' can tell, man:
It raises man aboon the brute,
    It mak's him ken himsel', man!
Gif ance the peasant taste a bit,
    He's greater than a lord, man,
And wi' the beggar shares a mite
    O' a' he can afford, man.

such

above

If

3

This fruit is worth a' Afric's wealth:
    To comfort us 'twas sent, man,
To gie the sweetest blush o' health,
    And mak' us a' content, man!
It clears the een, it cheers the heart,
    Mak's high and low guid friends, man,
And he wha acts the traitor's part,
    It to perdition sends, man.

eyes

4

My blessings ay attend the chiel,   *fellow*
   Wha pitied Gallia's slaves, man,
And staw a branch, spite o' the Deil,   *stole*
   Frae 'yont the western waves, man!   *beyond*
Fair Virtue water'd it wi' care,
   And now she sees wi' pride, man,
How weel it buds and blossoms there,
   It branches spreading wide, man.

5

But vicious folk ay hate to see
   The works o' Virtue thrive, man.
The courtly vermin's bann'd the tree,
   And grat to see it thrive, man!   *wept*
King Louis thought to cut it down,
   When it was unco sma', man;   *very*
For this the watchman crack'd his crown,
   Cut aff his head and a', man.

6

A wicked crew syne, on a time,   *then*
   Did tak' a solemn aith, man,   *oath*
It ne'er should flourish to its prime –
   I wat they pledg'd their faith, man!   *wot*
Awa they gaed wi' mock parade,   *went*
   Like beagles hunting game, man,
But soon grew weary o' the trade,
   And wish'd they'd been at hame, man.

7

Fair Freedom, standing by the tree,
   Her sons did loudly ca', man,

She sang a sang o' Liberty,
    Which pleas'd them ane and a', man.
By her inspir'd, the new-born race
    Soon drew the avenging steel, man.
gave   The hirelings ran – her foes gied chase,
    And bang'd the despot weel, man.

8

Let Britain boast her hardy oak,
    Her poplar, and her pine, man!
Auld Britain ance could crack her joke,
    And o'er her neighbours shine, man!
But seek the forest round and round,
    And soon 'twill be agreed, man,
That sic a tree can not be found
    'Twixt London and the Tweed, man.

9

Without this tree alake this life
    Is but a vale o' woe, man,
A scene o' sorrow mix'd wi' strife,
    Nae real joys we know, man;
We labour soon, we labour late,
    To feed the titled knave, man,
And a' the comfort we're to get,
beyond   Is that ayont the grave, man.

10

Wi' plenty o' sic trees, I trow,
    The warld would live in peace, man.
The sword would help to mak' a plough,
    The din o' war wad cease, man.
Like brethren in a common cause,

We'd on each other smile, man;
And equal rights and equal laws
   Wad gladden every isle, man.

11

Wae worth the loon what wadna eat   *woe befall the fellow*
   Sic halesome, dainty cheer, man
I'd gie the shoon frae aff my feet,
   To taste the fruit o't here, man!
Syne let us pray, Auld England may   *Then*
   Sure plant this far-famed tree, man;
And blythe we'll sing, and herald the day
   That gives us liberty, man.

At Carron Ironworks

We cam na here to view your warks   *not; works*
   In hopes to be mair wise,
But only, lest we gang to Hell,   *go*
   It may be nae surprise.
But when we tir'd at your door   *knocked*
   Your porter dought na bear us: *could not permit*
Sae may, should we to Hell's yetts come,   *gates*
   Your billie Satan sair us.   *fellow; serve*

On a Wag in Mauchline

1

Lament him, Mauchline husbands a',
  He aften did assist ye;
For had ye staid hale weeks awa',
  Your wives they ne'er had missed ye!

2

Ye Mauchline bairns, as on ye pass
  To school in bands thegither,
O, tread ye lightly on his grass –
  Perhaps he was your father!

Green Grow The Rashes, O

TUNE: (*As Title*)

Chorus

Green grow the rashes, O;
Green grow the rashes, O;
The sweetest hours that e'er I spend,
Are spent among the lasses, O.

1

There's nought but care on ev'ry han',
  In every hour that passes, O:
What signifies the life o' man,
  An' 'twere na for the lasses, O.

2

The war'ly race may riches chase,   *worldly*
   An' riches still may fly them, O;
An' tho' at last they catch them fast,
   Their hearts can ne'er enjoy them, O.

3

But gie me a cannie hour at e'en,   *quiet*
   My arms about my dearie, O,
An' war'ly cares an' war'ly men   *worldly*
   May a' gae tapsalteerie, O!   *topsy-turvy*

4

For you sae douce, ye sneer at this;   *grave*
   Ye're nought but senseless asses, O;
The wisest man the warl' e'er saw,   *world*
   He dearly love'd the lasses, O.

5

Auld Nature swears, the lovely dears
   Her noblest work she classes, O:
Her prentice han' she try'd on man,
   An' then she made the lasses, O.

O, Whistle An' I'll Come To Ye My Lad

TUNE: (As Title)

Chorus

O, whistle an' I'll come to ye, my lad!
O, whistle an' I'll come to ye, my lad!
Tho' father an' mother an' a' should gae mad,
O, whistle an' I'll come to ye, my lad!

go

1

But warily tent when ye come to court me,
And come nae unless the back-yett be a-jee;
Syne up the back-style, and let naebody see,
And come as ye were na comin to me,
And come as ye were na comin to me!

spy
not; -gate; ajar
Then
not

2

At kirk, or at market, when'er ye meet me,
Gang by me as tho' that ye car'd na a flie;
But steal me a blink o' your bonie black e'e,
Yet look as ye were na lookin to me,
Yet look as ye were na lookin to me!

Go: fly
glance

3

Ay vow and protest that ye care na for me,
And whyles ye may lightly my beauty a wee;
But court na anither tho' jokin ye be,
For fear that she wyle your fancy frae me,
For fear that she wyle your fancy frae me!

sometimes;
disparage; little

entice

167

MacPherson's Farewell

TUNE: *MacPherson's Rant*

Chorus

Sae rantingly, sae wantonly,   joivially
   Sae dauntingly gaed he,   went
He play'd a spring, and danc'd it round
   Below the gallows-tree.

1

Farewell, ye dungeons dark and strong,
   The wretch's destinie!
MacPherson's time will not be long
   On yonder gallows-tree.

2

O, what is death but parting breath?
   On many a bloody plain
I've dar'd his face, and in this place
   I scorn him yet again!

3

Untie these bands from off my hands,
   And bring to me my sword,
And there's no a man in all Scotland
   But I'll brave him at a word.

4

I've liv'd a life of sturt and strife;   trouble
   I die by treacherie:

It burns my heart I must depart,
  And not avengèd be.

5

Now farewell light, thou sunshine bright,
  And all beneath the sky!
May coward shame distain his name,
  The wretch that dare not die!

Ay Waukin, O

TUNE: (*As Title*)

Chorus

awake

Ay waukin, O,
  Waukin still and weary:
  Sleep I can get nane
  For thinking on my dearie.

1

Summer

Simmer's a pleasant time:
  Flowers of every colour,

crag

The water rins owre the heugh,
  And I long for my true lover.

2

When I sleep I dream,

apprehensive

When I wauk I'm eerie,

169

Sleep I can get nane
   For thinkin on my dearie.

3

Lanely night comes on,
   A' the lave are sleepin,   *rest*
I think on my bonie lad,
   And I bleer my een wi' greetin.   *eyes; weeping*

Of A' The Airts   *directions*

TUNE: *Miss Admiral Gordon's Strathspey*

1

Of a' the airts the wind can blaw
   I dearly like the west,
For there the bonie lassie lives,
   The lassie I lo'e best.
There wild woods grow, and rivers row,
   And monie a hill between,   *roll*
But day and night my fancy's flight
   Is ever wi' my Jean.

2

I see her in the dewy flowers –
   I see her sweet and fair.
I hear her in the tunefu' birds –
   I hear her charm the air.
There's not a bonie flower that springs

wood

By fountain, shaw, or green,
There's not a bonie bird that sings,

reminds

But minds me o' my Jean.

⁓

John Anderson My Jo

TUNE: (As Title)

1

John Anderson my jo, John,

acquainted

When we were first acquent,
Your locks were like the raven,

straight

Your bonie brow was brent;

bald

But now your brow is beld, John,
Your locks are like the snaw,

pate

But blessings on your frosty pow,
John Anderson my jo!

2

John Anderson my jo, John,

climbed; together

We clamb the hill thegither,
And monie a cantie day, John,

jolly

We've had wi' ane anither;

must

Now we maun totter down, John,
And hand in hand we'll go,
And sleep thegither at the foot,
John Anderson my jo!

Ca' the Yowes To The Knowes

Drive; ewes
knolls

TUNE: *Ca' the Yowes*

Chorus
Ca' the yowes to the knowes,
Ca' them whare the heather grows,
Ca' them whare the burnie rowes,   *brooklet; rolls*
  My bonie dearie!

1
As I gaed down the water-side,   *went*
There I met my shepherd lad:
He row'd me sweetly in his plaid,   *wrapped*
  And he ca'd me his dearie.   *called*

2
'Will ye gang down the water-side,
And see the waves sae sweetly glide   *go*
Beneath the hazels spreading wide,
  The moon it shines fu' clearly?

3
'I was bred up in nae sic school,   *such*
My shepherd lad, to play the fool,
An' a' the day to sit in dool,   *sorrow*
  An' naebody to see me'.

4
'Ye sall get gowns and ribbons meet,
Cauf-leather shoon upon your feet,   *Calf-*
And in my arms ye'se lie and sleep,
  An' ye sall be my dearie.'

5

I'll go

'If ye'll but stand to what ye've said,
I'se gang wi' you, my shepherd lad,
And ye may row me in your plaid,
   And I sall be your dearie.'

6

wind
shines; sky high

'While waters wimple to the sea,
While day blinks in the lift sae hie,
Till clay-cauld death sall blin' my e'e,
   Ye sall be my dearie.'

Ae Fond Kiss

TUNE: *Rory Dall's Port*

1

Ae fond kiss, and then we sever!
Ae farewell, and then forever!
Deep in heart-wrung tears I'll pledge thee,
Warring sighs and groans I'll wage thee.

2

Who shall say that Fortune grieves him,
While the star of hope she leaves him?
Me, nae cheerfu' twinkle lights me,
Dark despair around benights me.

3

I'll ne'er blame my partial fancy:
Naething could resist my Nancy!
But to see her was to love her,
Love but her, and love for ever.

4

Had we never lov'd sae kindly,
Had we never lov'd sae blindly,
Never met – or never parted –
We had ne'er been broken-hearted.

5

Fare-thee-weel, thou first and fairest!
Fare-thee-weel, thou best and dearest!
Thine be ilka joy and treasure,   *every*
Peace, Enjoyment, Love and Pleasure!

6

Ae fond kiss, and then we sever!
Ae farewell, alas, for ever!
Deep in heart-wrung tears I'll pledge thee,
Warring sighs and groans I'll wage thee.

Bonie Wee Thing

TUNE: (*As Title*)

Chorus

gentle

Bonie wee thing, cannie wee thing,
    Lovely wee thing, wert thou mine,
I wad wear thee in my bosom

lose

    Lest my jewel it should tine.

1

Wishfully I look and languish
    In that bonie face o' thine,

aches

And my heart it stounds wi' anguish,
    Lest my wee thing be na mine.

2

Wit and Grace and Love and Beauty

one

    In ae constellation shine!
To adore thee is my duty,
    Goddess o' this soul o' mine!

The Banks o' Doon

TUNE: *Caledonian Hunt's Delight*

1

Ye banks and braes o' bonie Doon,　　　　　*slopes*
　　How can ye bloom sae fresh and fair?
How can ye chant, ye little birds,
　　And I sae weary fu' o' care!
Thou'll break my heart, thou warbling bird,
　　That wantons thro' the flowering thorn!
Thou minds me o' departed joys,
　　Departed never to return.

2

Aft hae I rov'd by bonie Doon
　　To see the rose and woodbine twine,
And ilka bird sang o' its luve,　　　　　*every*
　　And fondly sae did I o' mine.
Wi' lightsome heart I pu'd a rose,　　　　*plucked*
　　Fu' sweet upon its thorny tree!
And my fause luver staw my rose –　　　　*stole*
　　But ah! he left the thorn wi' me.

A Parcel of Rogues in a Nation

TUNE: *(As Title)*

1

Fareweel to a' our Scottish fame,
  Fareweel our ancient glory!
Fareweel ev'n to the Scottish name,
  Sae famed in martial story!
Now Sark rins over Solway sands,
  An' Tweed rins to the ocean,
To mark where England's province stands –
  Such a parcel of rogues in a nation!

2

What force or guile could not subdue
  Thro' many warlike ages
Is wrought now by a coward few
  For hireling traitor's wages.
The English steel we could disdain,
  Secure in valour's station;
But English gold has been our bane –
  Such a parcel of rogues in a nation!

3

O, would, or I had seen the day
  That Treason thus could sell us,
My auld grey head had lien in clay
  Wi' Bruce and loyal Wallace!
But pith and power, till my last hour
  I 'll mak this declaration:–
'We're bought and sold for English gold' –
  Such a parcel of rogues in a nation!

Even when without

177

The Slave's Lament

TUNE: *(As Title)*

1

It was in sweet Senegal
That my foes did me enthral
 For the lands of Virginia, -ginia, O!
Torn from that lovely shore,
And must never see it more,
 And alas! I am weary, weary, O!

2

All on that charming coast
Is no bitter snow and frost,
 Like the lands of Virginia, -ginia O!
There streams for ever flow,
And the flowers for ever blow,
 And alas! I am weary, weary, O!

3

The burden I must bear,
While the cruel scourge I fear,
 In the lands of Virginia, -ginia, O!
 And I think on friends most dear
With the bitter, bitter tear,
 And alas! I am weary, weary, O!

Sweet Afton

TUNE: *Afton Water*

1

slopes

Flow gently, sweet Afton, among thy green braes!
Flow gently, I'll sing thee a song in thy praise!
My Mary's asleep by thy murmuring stream –
Flow gently, sweet Afton, disturb not her dream!

2

Thou stock dove whose echo resouds thro' the glen,
Ye wild whistling blackbirds in yon thorny den
Thou green-crested lapwing, thy screaming forbear –
I charge you, distub not my slumbering fair!

3

How lofty, sweet Afton, thy neighbouring hills,
Farm mark'd with the courses of clear, winding rills!
There daily I wander, as noon rises high,
My flocks and my Mary's sweet cot in my eye.

4

How pleasant thy banks and green vallies below,
Where wild in the woodlands the primroses blow:
There oft, as mild ev'ning weeps over the lea.

birch

The sweet-scented birk shades my Mary and me.

5

Thy crystal stream, Afton, how lovely it glides,
And winds by the cot where my Mary resides!

179

How wanton thy waters her snowy feet lave,
As, gathering sweet flowerets, she stems thy clear
    wave!

6

Flow gently, sweet Afton, among thy green braes!
Flow gently, sweet river, the theme of my lays!
My Mary's asleep by thy murmuring stream –
Flow gently, sweet Afton, distub not her dream!

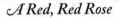

A Red, Red Rose

TUNE: Major Graham

1

O, my luve's like a red, red rose,
    That's newly sprung in June.
O, my luve's like the melodie,
    That's sweetly play'd in tune.

2

As fair art thou, my bonie lass,
    So deep in luve am I,
And I will luve thee still, my Dear,
    Till a' the seas gang dry.

go

3

Till a' the seas gang dry, my Dear,
  And the rocks melt wi' the sun!
O I will luve thee still, my Dear,
  While the sands o' life shall run.

4

And fare thee weel, my only Luve,
  And fare what weel a while!
And I will come again, my Luve,
  Tho' it were ten thousand mile!

⌒⌒⌒

old long ago

Auld Lang Syne

TUNE: (As Title)

Chorus
And for auld lang syne, my jo,
For auld lang syne,
We'll tak a cup o' kindness yet,
For auld lang syne.

1

Should auld acquaintance be forgot,
  And never brought to mind?
Should auld acquaintance be forgot,
  And days o' lang syne?

2

And surely ye'll be your pint-stowp!   *pay for*
   And surely I'll be mine!
And we'll tak a cup o' kindness yet,
   For auld lang syne.

3

We twa hae run about the braes   *hillsides*
   And pu'd the gowans fine: *pulled; wild daisies*
But we've wander'd mony a weary foot
   Sin auld lang syne.   *since*

4

We twa hae paidl'd i' the burn,   *waded; brook*
   Frae mornin' sun till dine;   *noon*
But seas between us braid hae roar'd   *broad*
   Sin auld lang syne.

5

And there's a hand, my trusty fiere!   *chum*
   And gie's a hand o' thine!   *give me*
And we'll tak a right gude-willy waught,   *good-will drink*
   For auld lang syne.

Comin Thro' The Rye

TUNE: Miller's Wedding

Chorus

wet; creature

O Jenny's a' weet, poor body,
Jenny's seldom dry:

draggled

She draigl't a' her petticoatie,
Comin thro' the rye!

1

Comin thro' the rye, poor body,
 Comin thro' the rye,
She draigl't a' her petticoatie,
 Comin thro' the rye!

2

Should

Gin a body meet a body
 Comin thro' the rye
Gin a body kiss a body,
 Need a body cry?

3

Gin a body meet a body
 Comin thro' the glen,
Gin a body kiss a body,
 Need the warld ken?

4

Gin a body meet a body
 Comin thro' the grain;
Gin a body kiss a body,
 The thing's a body's ain.

Charlie He's My Darling

TUNE: *(As Title)*

Chorus
An' Charlie he's my darling,
My darling, my darling,
Charlie he's my darling -
The Young Chevalier!

1

'Twas on a Monday morning
    Right early in the year,
That Charlie came to our town -
    The Young Chevalier!

2

As he was walking up the street
    The city for to view,
O, there he spied a bonie lass
    The window looking thro'!

3

Sae light's he jimpèd up the stair,
    And tirl'd at the pin;
And wha sae ready as hersel'
    To let the laddie in!

rasped

4

He set his Jenny on his knee,
    All in his Highland dress;
For brawlie weel he kend the way
    To please a bonie lass.

finely well

5

It's up yon heathery mountain
    And down yon scroggy glen,
We daurna gang a-milking
    For Charlie and his men!

wet; creature

daren't go

Scots, Wha Hae

TUNE: *Hey, tutti taitie*

1

Scots, wha hae wi' Wallace bled,
Scots, wham Bruce has aften led,
Welcome to your gory bed
            Or to victorie!

2

Now's the day, and now's the hour:
See the front o' battle lour,
See approach proud Edward's power –
            Chains and slaverie!

3

Wha will be a traitor knave?
Wha can fill a coward's grave?
Wha sae base as be a slave? –
            Let him turn, and flee!

4

Wha for Scotland's King and Law
Freedom's sword will strongly draw,
Freeman stand or freeman fa',
    Let him follow me!

5

By Oppression's woes and pains,
By your sons in servile chains,
We will drain our dearest veins
    But they shall be free!

6

Lay the proud usurpers low!
Tyrants fall in every foe!
Liberty's in every blow!
    Let us do, or die!

Highland Mary

TUNE: *Lady Catherine Ogle*

1

Ye banks and braes and streams around
 The castle o' Montgomery,
Green be your woods, and fair your flowers,
 Your waters never drumlie!   turbid
There Summer first unfald her robes,   unfold
 And there the langest tarry!

For there I took the last fareweel
  O' my sweet Highland Mary!

2

birch

How sweetly bloom'd the gay, green birk,
  How rich the hawthorn's blossom,
As underneath their fragrant shade
  I clasp'd her to my bosom!
The golden hours on angel wings
  Flew o'er me and my dearie:
For dear to me as light and life
  Was my sweet Highland Mary.

3

Wi' monie a vow and lock'd embrace
  Our parting was fu' tender;
And, pledging aft to meet again,
  We tore oursels asunder.
But O, fell Death's untimely frost,
  That nipt my flower sae early!
Now green's the sod, and cauld's the clay,
  That wraps my Highland Mary!

4

O, pale, pale now, those rosy lips
  I aft hae kiss'd sae fondly;
And clos'd for ay, the sparkling glance
  That dwalt on me sae kindly;
And mouldering now in silent dust
  That heart that lo'ed me dearly!
But still within my bosom's core
  Shall live my Highland Mary.

Ca' The Yowes to the Knowes

TUNE: *Ca' the Yowes*

Second Set

Chorus
Ca' the yowes to the knowes,
Ca' them where the heather grows,
Ca' them where the burnie rowes,   brooklet runs
   My bonie dearie.

1
Hark, the mavis' e'ening sang
Sounding Clouden's woods amang,
Then a-faulding let us gang,   go
   My bonie dearie.

2
We'll gae down by Clouden side,
Thro' the hazels, spreading wide
O'er the waves that sweetly glide
   To the moon sae clearly.

3
Yonder Clouden's silent towers,
Where, at moonshine's midnight hours,
O'er the dewy bending flowers
   Fairies dance sae cheery.

4
Ghaist nor bogle shalt thou fear –   hobgoblin
Thou'rt to Love and Heav'n sae dear

Nocht of ill may come thee near,
　　My bonie dearie.

5

Fair and lovely as thou art,
Thou hast stown my very heart;
I can die – but canna part,
　　My bonie dearie.

stolen

～～～

Is There For Honest Poverty

TUNE: *For a' that*

1

Is there for honest poverty
　　That hings his head, an' a' that?
The coward slave, we pass him by –
　　We dare be poor for a' that!
For a' that, an' a' that,
　　Our toils obscure, an' a' that,
The rank is but the guinea's stamp,
　　The man's the gowd for a' that.

hangs

gold

2

What though on hamely fare we dine,
　　Wear hoddin grey, an' a' that?
Gie fools their silks, and knaves their wine –
　　A man's a man for a' that.

coarse grey woollen

189

For a' that, an' a' that,
    Their tinsel show, an' a' that,
The honest man, tho' e'er sae poor,
    Is king o' men for a' that.

3

Ye see yon birkie ca'd 'a lord,'   *fellow; called*
    Wha struts, an' stares, an' a' that?
ho' hundreds worship at his word,
    He's but a cuif for a' that.   *dolt*
For a' that, an' a' that,
    His ribband, star, an' a' that,
The man o' independent mind,
    He looks an' laughs at a' that.

4

A prince can mak a belted knight,
    A marquis, duke, an' a' that!
But an honest man's aboon his might –   *above*
    Guid faith, he mauna fa' that!   *must not*
For a' that, an' a' that,
    Their dignities, an' a' that,
The pith o' sense an' pride o' worth
    Are higher rank than a' that.

5

Then let us pray that come it may
    (As come it will for a' that)
That Sense and Worth o'er a' the earth
    Shall bear the gree an' a' that!   *have the first place*
For a' that, an' a' that!
    It's comin yet for a' that,

That man to man the world o'er
Shall brithers be for a' that.

O Let Me in This Ae Night

TUNE: *Will ye lend me your loom, lass?*

Chorus
O, let me in this ae night,
This ae, ae, ae night!
O, let me in this ae night,
And rise, and let me in!

1

O lassie, are ye sleepin yet,
Or are ye waukin, I wad wit?
For Love has bound me hand an' fit,
    And I would fain be in, jo.

2

Thou hear'st the winter wind an' weet:
Nae star blinks thro' the driving sleet!
Tak pity on my weary feet,
    And shield me frae the rain, jo.

3

The bitter blast that round me blaws,
Unheeded howls, unheeded fa's:
The cauldness o' thy heart's the cause
    Of a' my care and pine, jo.

one

awake; know
foot

wet
shines

HER ANSWER

Chorus
I tell you now this ae night,
This ae, ae, ae night,
And ance for a' this ae night,
I winna let ye in, jo.   will not

1

O, tell me na o' wind an' rain,   not
Upbraid na me wi' cauld disdain,
Gae back the gate ye cam again,   way
  I winna let ye in, jo!

2

The snellest blast at mirkest hours,   keenest; darkest
That round the pathless wand'rer pours
Is nocht to what poor she endures,   nothing
  That's trusted faithless man, jo.

3

The sweetest flower that deck'd the mead,
Now trodden like the vilest weed –
Let simple maid the lesson read!
The weird may be her ain, jo.   fate; own

4

The bird that charm'd his summer day,
And now the cruel fowler's prey,
Let that to witless woman say:–
'The gratefu' heart of man,' jo.

Mary Morison

TUNE: *Duncan Davison*

1

O Mary, at thy window be!
   It is the wish'd, the trysted hour.
Those smiles and glances let me see,
   That make the miser's treasure poor.

bear the struggle   How blythely wad I bide the stoure,
A weary slave frae sun to sun,
   Could I the rich reward secure –
The lovely Mary Morison!

2

Last night   Yestreen, when to the trembling string
went   The dance gaed thro' the lighted ha',
To thee my fancy took its wing,
   I sat, but neither heard or saw:
fine   Tho' this was fair, and that was braw,
the other   And yon the toast of a' the town,
   I sigh'd and said amang them a':–
'Ye are na Mary Morison!'

3

O Mary, canst thou wreck his peace
   What for thy sake wad gladly die?
Or canst thou break that heart of his
fault   Whase only faut is loving thee?
give   If love for love thou wilt na gie,
   At least be pity to me shown:
cannot   A thought ungentle canna be
The thought o' Mary Morison.

193

O Leave Novéls

TUNE: *Donald Blue*

1

O, leave novéls, ye Mauchline belles –
    Ye're safer at your spinning-wheel!
Such witching books are baited hooks
    For rakish rooks like Rob Mossgiel.

2

Your fine *Tom Jones* and *Grandisons*
    They make your youthful fancies reel!
They heat your brains, and fire your veins,
    And then you're prey for Rob Mossgiel.

3

Beware a tongue that's smoothly hung,
    A heart that warmly seems to feel!
That feeling heart but acts a part –
    'Tis rakish art in Rob Mossgiel.

4

The frank address, the soft caress
    Are worse than poisoned darts of steel:
The frank address and politesse
    Are all finesse in Rob Mossgiel.

There Was A Lad

TUNE: *Dainty Davie*

Chorus
Robin was a rovin boy,
Rantin, rovin, rantin, rovin,
Robin was a rovin boy,
Rantin, rovin Robin!

roystering

1

There was a lad was born in Kyle,
But whatna day o' whatna style,
I doubt it's hardly worth the while
    To be sae nice wi' Robin.

what

2

Our monarch's hindmost year but ane
Was five-and-twenty days begun,
'Twas then a blast o' Janwar' win'
    Blew hansel in on Robin.

one

January wind

3

The gossip keekit in his loof,
Quo' scho:– 'Wha lives will see the proof,
This waly boy will be nae coof:
    I think we'll ca' him Robin.

glanced; palm
Quoth she
thumping; dolt

4

'He'll hae misfortunes great an' sma',
But ay a heart aboon them a'.
He'll be a credit till us a':
    We'll a' be proud o' Robin!

above

to

195

5

'But sure as three times three mak nine,
I see by ilka score and line,   *every kind*
This chap will dearly like our kin',
    So leeze me on thee, Robin!   *Commend me to*

6

'Guid faith,' quo' scho, 'I doubt you gar   *make*
The bonie lasses lie aspar;   *aspread*
But twenty fauts ye may hae waur –   *faults; worse*
    So blessins on thee, Robin!'

✦

The Lass o' Ballochmyle

TUNE: *Ettrick Banks*

1

'Twas even: the dewy fields were green,
  On every blade the pearls hang,   *hung*
The zephyr wanton'd round the bean,
    And bore its fragrant sweets alang,
    In ev'ry glen the mavis sang,
All Nature list'ning seem'd the while,
  Except where greenwood echoes rang
Amang the braes o' Ballochmyle.   *heights*

2

With careless step I onward stray'd,

My heart rejoic'd in Nature's joy,
When, musing in a lonely glade,
    A maiden fair I chanc'd to spy.
    Her look was like the Morning's eye,
Her air like Nature's vernal smile.
    Perfection whisper'd, passing by:–
'Behold the lass o' Ballochmyle!'

3

Fair is the morn in flowery May,
    And sweet is night in autumn mild,
When roving thro' the garden gay,
    Or wand'ring in the lonely wild;
    But woman, Nature's darling child –
There all her charms she does compile!
    Even there her other works are foil'd
By the bonie lass o' Ballochmyle.

4

O, had she been a country maid,
    And I the happy country swain,
Tho' shelter'd in the lowest shed
    That ever rose on Scotia's plain,
    Thro' weary winter's wind and rain
With joy, with rapture, I would toil,
    And nightly to my bosom strain
The bonie lass o' Ballochmyle!

5

Then Pride might climb the slipp'ry steep,
    Where fame and honours lofty shine,
And thirst of gold might tempt the deep,

Or downward seek the Indian mine!
Give me the cot below the pine,
To tend the flocks or till the soil,
And ev'ry day have joys divine
With the bonie lass o' Ballochmyle.

O, Wert Thou in the Cauld Blast

TUNE: *Lennox love to Blantyre*

1

O, wert thou in the cauld blast
    On yonder lea, on yonder lea,
My plaidie to the angry airt,   plaid; quarter
    I'd shelter thee, I'd shelter thee.
Or did Misfortune's bitter storms
    Around thee blaw, around thee blaw.
Thy bield should be my bosom,   shelter
    To share it a', to share it a'.

2

Or were I in the wildest waste,
    Sae black and bare, sae black and bare,
The desert were a Paradise,
    If thou wert there, if thou wert there.
Or were I monarch of the globe,
    Wi' thee to reign, wi' thee to reign,
The brightest jewel in my crown
    Wad be my queen, wad be my queen

Scotch Drink

Gie him strong drink until he wink,
That 's sinking in despair;
An' liquor guid to fire his bluid,
That's prest wi' grief an' care:
There let him bowse, and deep carouse,
Wi' bumpers flowing o'er,
Till he forgets his loves or debts,
An' minds his griefs no more.

Solomon's Proverbs, xxxi. 6, 7.

1

Let other poets raise a frácas
'Bout vines, an' wines, an' drucken Bacchus,
An' crabbit names an' stories wrack us,
   An' grate our lug:
I sing the juice Scotch bear can mak us,
   In glass or jug.

2

O thou, my Muse! guid auld Scotch drink!
Whether thro' wimplin worms thou jink,
Or, richly brown, ream owre the brink,
   In glorious faem,
Inspire me, till I lisp an' wink,
   To sing thy name!

3

Let husky wheat the haughs adorn,
An' aits set up their awnie horn,

199

An' pease an' beans, at e'en or morn,
    Perfume the plain:
Leeze me on thee, John Barleycorn,   *Blessings on thee*
    Thou king o' grain!

4

On thee aft Scotland chows her cood,   *chews cud*
In souple scones, the wale o' food!   *pick*
Or tumbling in the boiling flood
    Wi' kail an' beef;   *greens*
But when thou pours thy strong heart's blood,
    There thou shines chief.

5

Food fills the wame, an' keeps us livin;   *belly*
Tho' life 's a gift no worth receivin,
When heavy-dragg'd wi' pine an' grievin;
    But oil'd by thee,
The wheels o' life gae down-hill, scrievin,   *careering*
    Wi' rattlin glee.

6

Thou clears the head o' doited Lear,   *muddled*
Thou cheers the heart o' drooping Care;   *Learning*
Thou strings the nerves o' Labour sair,
    At's weary toil;
Thou ev'n brightens dark Despair
    Wi' gloomy smile.

7

Aft, clad in massy siller weed,   *dress*
Wi' gentles thou erects thy head;

Yet, humbly kind in time o' need,
      The poor man's wine:

porridge

His wee drap parritch, or his bread,
      Thou kitchens fine.

8

Thou art the life o' public haunts:

Without; merry-makings

But thee, what were our fairs and rants?
Ev'n godly meetings o' the saunts,
      By thee inspir'd,
When, gaping, they besiege the tents,
      Are doubly fir'd.

9

That merry night we get the corn in,
O sweetly, then, thou reams the horn in!

smoking
wooden vessels

Or reekin on a New-Year mornin
      In cog or bicker

whisky

An' just a wee drap sp'ritual burn in,

tasty sugar

      An' gusty sucker!

10

When Vulcan gies his bellows breath,

gear

An' ploughmen gather wi' their graith,

froth

O rare! to see thee fizz an' freath

two-eared cup

I' th' lugget caup!

the Black-smith

Then Burnewin comes on like death

stroke

At ev'ry chaup.

11

iron

Nae mercy, then, for airn or steel:

bony, fellow

The brawnie, bainie, ploughman chiel,
Brings hard owrehip, wi' sturdy wheel,

The strong forehammer,
Till block an' studdie ring an' reel,   anvil
       Wi' dinsome clamour

12

When skirlin weanies see the light,   squalling
Thou maks the gossips clatter bright,   babies babble
How fumbling cuifs their dearies slight;   cheerfully dolts
       Wae worth the name!   Woe befall
Nae howdie gets a social night,   midwife
       Or plack frae them.   coin

13

When neebors anger at a plea,   law-case
An' just as wud as wud can be,   wild
How easy can the barley-brie   -brew
       Cement the quarrel!
It's aye the cheapest lawyer's fee,
       To taste the barrel.

14

Alake! that e'er my Muse has reason,
To wyte her countrymen wi' treason!   charge
But monie daily weet their weason   throat
       Wi' liquors nice,
An' hardly, in a winter season,
       E'er spier her price.   ask

15

Wae worth that brandy, burnin trash!
Fell source o' monie a pain an' brash!   illness
Twins monie a poor, doylt, drucken hash,   robs; stupid,
       O' half his days;   drunken oaf

An' sends, beside, auld Scotland's cash
foes   To her warst faes.

16

Ye Scots, wha wish auld Scotland well!
Ye chief, to you my tale I tell,
penniless   Poor, plackless devils like mysel!
becomes   It sets you ill,
meddle   Wi' bitter, dearthfu' wines to mell,
                  Or foreign gill.

17

bladder   May gravels round his blather wrench,
      An' gouts torment him, inch by inch,
face; growl   Wha twists his gruntle wi' a glunch
               O' sour disdain,
      Out owre a glass o' whisky-punch
               Wi' honest men!

18

O Whisky! soul o' plays an' pranks!
Accept a Bardie's gratefu' thanks!
creakings   When wanting thee, what tuneless cranks
              Are my poor verses!
Thou comes – they rattle i' their ranks
            At ither's arses!

19

Thee, Ferintosh! O sadly lost!
Scotland lament frae coast to coast!
cough   Now colic grips, an' barkin hoast
              May kill us a';

For loyal Forbés' chartered boast
            Is taen awa!

20

Thae curst horse-leeches o' th' Excise,   Those
Wha mak the whisky stells their prize!   stills
Haud up thy han', Deil! ance, twice, thrice!
            There, seize the blinkers!   spies
An' bake them up in brustane pies   brimstone
            For poor damn'd drinkers.

21

Fortune! if thou'll but gie me still
Hale breeks, a scone, an' whisky gill,   Whole breeches store
An' rowth o' rhyme to rave at will,
            Tak a' the rest,
An' deal't about as thy blind skill
            Directs thee best.

<hr />

Poor Mailie's Elegy

1

Lament in rhyme, lament in prose,
Wi' saut tears tricklin down your nose;
Our Bardie's fate is at a close,
            Past a' remead!   remedy
The last, sad cape-stane of his woes;   keystone
            Poor Mailie's dead!

2

worldly wealth

It's no the loss o' warl's gear,
That could sae bitter draw the tear,

drooping

Or mak our Bardie, dowie, wear
        The mourning weed:
He's lost a friend an' neebor dear
        In Mailie dead.

3

farm

Thro' a' the toun she trotted by him;
A lang half-mile she could descry him;
Wi' kindly bleat, when she did spy him,
        She ran wi' speed:
A friend mair faithfu' ne'er cam nigh him,
        Than Mailie dead.

4

know

I wat she was a sheep o' sense,

tact

An' could behave hersel' wi' mense:
I'll say't, she never brak a fence,
        Thro' thievish greed.

parlour

Our Bardie, lanely, keeps the spence
        Sin' Mailie's dead.

5

glen

Or, if he wanders up the howe,
Her livin image in her yowe

knoll

Comes bleatin till him, owre the knowe,
        For bits o' bread;

roll

An' down the briny pearls rowe
        For Mailie dead.

6

She was nae get o' moorlan tips,	issue; rams
Wi' tawted ket, an' hairy hips;	matted fleece; rumps
For her forbears were brought in ships,	ancestors
Frae 'yont the Tweed:	
A bonier fleesh ne'er cross'd the clips	fleece; shears
Than Mailie's dead.	

7

Wae worth the man wha first did shape	Woe befall
That vile, wanchancie thing – a rape!	dangerous
It maks guid fellows girn an' gape,	grin
Wi' chokin dread;	
An' Robin's bonnet wave wi' crape	
For Mailie dead.	

8

O a' ye bards on bonie Doon!	
An' wha on Ayr your chanters tune!	bagpipes
Come, join the melancholious croon	
O' Robin's reed!	
His heart will never get aboon!	rejoice
His Mailie's dead!	

A Dream

Thoughts, words, and deeds, the Statute blames with reason;
But surely Dreams *were ne'er indicted Treason.*

On reading in the public papers, the Laureate's Ode with the other parade of June 4th, 1786, the Author was no sooner dropt asleep, than he imagined himself transported to the Birth-day Levee: and, in his dreaming fancy, made the following Address:

1

Guid-morning to your Majesty!
    May Heaven augment your blisses,
On ev'ry new birth-day ye see,
    A humble Poet wishes!
My Bardship here, at your Levee,
    On sic a day as this is,
Is sure an uncouth sight to see,
    Amang thae birth-day dresses
        Sae fine this day.

those

2

I see ye're complimented thrang,
    By monie a lord an' lady;
God Save the King's a cuckoo sang
    That's unco easy said ay:
The poets, too, a venal gang,
    Wi' rhymes well-turn'd an' ready,
Wad gar you trow ye ne'er do wrang,
    But ay unerring steady,
        On sic a day.

busily

mighty

make; think

3

For me! before a Monarch's face,
   Ev'n there I winna flatter;
For neither pension, post, nor place,
   Am I your humble debtor:
So, nae reflection on your Grace,
   Your Kingship to bespatter;
There's monie waur been o' the race,   *worse*
   And aiblins ane been better   *maybe*
          Than you this day.

4

'Tis very true my sovereign King,
   My skill may weel be doubted;
But facts are chiels that winna ding,   *fellows; be upset*
   And downa be disputed: *cannot*
Your royal nest, beneath your wing,
   Is e'en right reft and clouted,   *torn and patched*
And now the third part o' the string,
   An' less, will gang about it
          Than did ae day.

5

Far be't frae me that I aspire
   To blame your legislation,
Or say, ye wisdom want, or fire
   To rule this mighty nation:
But faith! I muckle doubt, my sire,   *greatly*
   Ye've trusted ministration
To chaps wha in a barn or byre   *cow-shed*
   Wad better fill'd their station,   *Would have*
          Than courts yon day.

6

And now ye've gien auld Britain peace,
    Her broken shins to plaister;
Your sair taxation does her fleece,
sixpence   Till she has scarce a tester:
For me, thank God, my life's a lease,
    Nae bargain wearin faster,
Or faith! I fear, that, wi' the geese,
behove   I shortly boost to pasture
croft   I' the craft some day.

7

I'm no mistrusting Willie Pitt,
    When taxes he enlarges,
breed   (An' Will's a true guid fallow's get,
spatters   A name not envy spairges,)
That he intends to pay your debt,
    An' lessen a' your charges;
But, God sake! let nae saving fit
    Abridge your bonie barges
                An' boats this day.

8

sport   Adieu, my Liege! may Freedom geck
    Beneath your high protection;
wring   An' may ye rax Corruption's neck,
    And gie her for dissection!
But since I'm here I'll no neglect,
    In loyal, true affection,
To pay your Queen, wi' due respect,
    My fealty an' subjection
                This great brith-day.

9

Hail, Majesty most Excellent!
   While nobles strive to please ye,
Will ye accept a compliment,
   A simple Bardie gies ye?
Thae bonie bairntime Heav'n has lent,   brood
   Still higher may they heeze ye   hoist
In bliss, till Fate some day is sent,
   For ever to release ye
            Frae care that day.

10

For you, young Potentate' o' Wales,
   I tell your Highness fairly,
Down Pleasure's stream wi' swelling sails,
   I'm tauld ye're driving rarely;
But some day ye may gnaw your nails,
   An' curse your folly sairly,
That e'er ye brak Diana's pales,   broke
   Or rattl'd dice wi' Charlie
            By night or day.

11

Yet aft a ragged cowte's been known,   colt
   To make a noble aiver;   old horse
So, ye may doucely fill a throne,   sedately
   For a' their clish-ma-claver: gossip
There, him at Agincourt wha shone,
   Few better were or braver;
And yet, wi' funny, queer Sir John,
   He was an unco shaver
            For monie a day.

12

For you, right rev'rend Osnaburg,
    Nane sets the lawn-sleeve sweeter,
becomes
ear
Altho' a ribban at your lug
    Wad been a dress completer:
haughty
As ye disown yon paughty dog,
    That bears the keys of Peter,
haste!
Then swith! an' get a wife to hug,
    Or trowth, ye'll stain the mitre
            Some luckless day!

13

Young, royal Tarry-breeks, I learn,
    Ye've lately come athwart her –
A glorious galley, stem an' stern
    Weel rigg'd for Venus' barter;
But first hang out that she'll discern
    Your hymeneal charter;
grappling-iron
Then heave aboard your grapple-airn,
    An', large upon her quarter,
            Come full that day.

14

Ye, lastly, bonie blossoms a',
    Ye royal lasses dainty,
Heav'n mak you guid as weel as braw,
    An' gie you lads a-plenty!
But sneer na British boys awa!
    For kings are unco scant ay,
An' German gentles are but sma':
    They're better just than want ay
            On onie day.

15

God bless you a'! consider now,
  Ye're unco muckle dautet;   *extremely; petted*
But ere the course o' life be through,
  It may be bitter sautet: *salted*
An' I hae seen their coggie fou,   *dish*
  That yet hae tarrow't at it;   *tarried*
But or the day was done, I trow,
  The laggen they hae clautet   *bottom; scraped*
        Fu' clean that day.

~~~

Halloween

Yes! let the rich deride, the proud disdain,
The simple pleasures of the lowly train:
To me more dear, congenial to my heart,
One native charm, than all the gloss of art.
                GOLDSMITH

1

Upon that night, when fairies light
  On Cassilis Downans dance,
Or owre the lays, in splendid blaze,   *partures*
  On sprightly coursers prance;
Or for Colean the rout is ta'en,   *road*
  Beneath the moon's pale beams;

There, up the Cove, to stray and rove,
    Amang the rocks and streams
        To sport that night:

2

Amang the bonie winding banks,
    Where Doon rings, wimplin, clear;
Where Bruce ance ruled the martial ranks,
    An' shook his Carrick spear;
Some merry, friendly, country-folks
    Together did convene,
To burn their nits, an' pou their stocks,
    An' haud their Hallowe'en
        Fu' blythe that night.

3

The lasses feat an' cleanly neat,
    Mair braw than when they're fine;
Their faces blythe fu' sweetly kythe
    Hearts leal, an' warm, an' kin':
The lads sae trig, wi' wooer-babs
    Weel-knotted on their garten;
Some unco blate, an' some wi' gabs
    Gar lasses' hearts gang startin
        Whyles fast at night.

4

Then, first an' foremost, thro' the kail,
    Their stocks maun a' be sought ance;
They steek their een, an' grape an' wale
    For muckle anes, an' straught anes.
Poor hav'rel Will fell aff the drift,

(marginal glosses)
- winding
- nuts; pull; plants
- keep
- spruce
- fair
- show
- loyal; kind
- love-knots
- garters
- shy; talk
- Sometimes
- shut; eyes; grope; choose
- big; straight
- foolish; lost the way

213

An' wandered thro' the bow-kail,   *cabbage*
An' pow't, for want o' better shift,   *pulled; choice*
  A runt, was like a sow-tail,   *stalk*
      Sae bow't that night.   *bent*

5

Then, straught or crooked, yird or nane,   *mould*
  They roar an' cry a' throu'ther;   *pell-mell*
The vera wee-things, toddling, rin   *children; run*
  Wi' stocks out-owre their shouther: *upon*
An' gif the custock 's sweet or sour,   *if; pith*
  Wi' joctelegs they taste them;   *pocket-knives*
Syne coziely, aboon the door,   *Then; above*
  Wi' cannie care, they 've plac'd them   *prudent*
      To lie that night.

6

The lasses staw frae 'mang them a',   *stole*
  To pou their stalks o' corn;
But Rab slips out, an' jinks about,   *dodges*
  Behint the muckle thorn:
He grippet Nelly hard an' fast;
  Loud skirl'd a' the lasses;   *squeaked*
But her tap-pickle maist was lost,
  Whan kiutlin in the fause-house   *cuddling*
      Wi' him that night.

7

The auld guid-wife's weel-hoorded nits   *well-hoarded*
  Are round an' round divided,
An' monie lads' an' lasses' fates
  Are there that night decided:

comfortably

Some kindle couthie, side by side,
    An' burn thegither trimly;
Some start awa wi' saucy pride,

fire-place

    An' jump out-owre the chimlie
        Fu' high that night.

8

watchful

Jean slips in twa, wi' tentie e'e;
    Wha 'twas, she wadna tell;
But this is *Jock*, an' this is me,

whispers

    She says in to hersel:
He bleez'd owre her, an' she owre him,
    As they wad never mair part;

chimney

Till fuff! he started up the lum,
    And Jean had e'en a sair heart
        To see't that night.

9

Poor Willie, wi' his bow-kail runt,

precise Molly

    Was burn wi' primsie Mallie;

huff

An' Mary, nae doubt, took the drunt,
    To be compar'd to Willie:

leaped; start

Mall's nit lap out, wi' pridefu' fling,

foot

    An' her ain fit, it burn it;
While Willie lap, an' swoor by jing,
    'Twas just the way he wanted
        To be that night.

10

Nell had the fause-house in her min',
    She pits hersel an' Rob in;
In loving bleeze they sweetly join.

215

Till white in ase they're sobbin: *ashes*
  Nell's heart was dancin at the view;
She whisper'd Rob to leuk for't:
  Rob, stownlins, prie'd her bonie mou,   *by stealth, tasted;*
                         mouth
  Fu' cozie in the neuk for't,   *corner*
            Unseen that night.

11

But Merran sat behint their back   *Marian*
  Her thoughts on Andrew Bell;
She lea'es them gashing at their cracks,   *grabbing*
  An' slips out by hersel:
She thro' the yard the nearest taks,
  An' to the kiln she goes then,
An' darklins grapit for the bauks,   *in the dark;*
    And in the blue-clue throwns then, *cross-beams*
            Right fear't that night.

12

An' ay she win't, an' ay she swat –   *wound; sweated*
  I wat she made nae jaukin;   *bet; trifling*
Till something held within the pat,   *kiln-pot*
  Guid Lord! but she was quakin!
But whether 'twas a bauk-en',   *beam-end*
  Or whether it was Andrew Bell,
She did na wait on talkin
          To spier that night.   *ask*

13

Wee Jenny to her graunie says,
  'Will ye go wi' me, graunie?
I'll eat the apple at the glass,

I gat frae uncle Johnie':

puffed; smoke She fuff't her pipe wi' sic a lunt,
  In wrath she was sae vap'rin,
cinder burnt She notic't na an aizle brunt
worsted Her braw, new, worset apron
        Out thro' that night.

14

'Ye little skelpie-limmer's-face!
  I daur ye try sic sportin,
Devil As seek the Foul Thief onie place,
  For him to spae your fortune:
tell Nae doubt but ye may get a sight!
  Great cause ye hae to fear it;
For monie a ane has gotten a fright,
mad An' liv'd an' died deleeret,
        On sic a night.

15

harvest; 'Ae hairst afore the Sherra-moor,
Sheriffmuir I mind't as weel's yestreen –
remember
young girl I was a gilpey then, I'm sure
  I was na past fyfteen:
The simmer had been cauld an' wat,
grain; very An' stuff was unco green;
rollicking An' ay a rantin kirn we gat,
harvest-home An' just on Halloween
        It fell that night.

16

chief harvester 'Our stibble-rig was Rab M'Graen,
  A clever, sturdy fallow;

217

His sin gat Eppie Sim wi' wean, _son; child_
    That lived in Achmachalla:
He gat hemp-seed, I mind it well,
    An' he made unco light o't;
But monie a day was by himself, _off his wits_
    He was sae sairly frightened
        That vera night.'

17

Then up gat fechtin Jamie Fleck, _fighting_
    An' he swoor by his conscience,
That he could saw hemp-seed a peck; _sow_
    For it was a' but nonsense: _all merely_
The auld guidman raught down the pock, _reached; bag_
    An' out a handfu' gied him;
Syne bad him slip frae 'mang the folk,
    Sometime when nae ane see'd him,
        An' try't that night.

18

He marches thro' amang the stacks,
    Tho' he was something sturtin; _staggered_
The graip he for a harrow taks, _dungfork_
    And haurls at his curpin; _trails; crupper_
And ev'ry now and then, he says,
    'Hemp-seed I saw thee, _sow_
An' her that is to be my lass
    Come after me, an' draw thee
        As fast this night'.

19

He whistl'd up *Lord Lenox' March*,
　　To keep his courage cheery;
Altho' his hair began to arch,
　　He was sae fley'd an' eerie;　　*scared; awe-stricken*
Till presently he hears a squeak,
　　An' then a grane an' gruntle;　　*groan*
He by his shouther gae a keek,　　*round; look*
　　An' tumbl'd wi' a wintle　　*somersault*
　　　　　　Out-owre that night.

20

He roar'd a horrid murder-shout,
　　In dreadfu' desperation!
An' young an' auld come rinning out,
　　An' hear the sad narration:
He swoor 'twas hilchin Jean M'Craw,　　*halting*
　　Or crouchie Merran Humphie –　　*hunchbacked*
Till stop! she trotted thro' them a';
　　An' wha was it but grumphie　　*the pig*
　　　　　　Asteer that night?　　*Astir*

21

Meg fain wad to the barn gaen,　　*have gone*
　　To winn three wechts o' naething;　　*winnow*
But for to meet the Deil her lane,　　*all by herself*
　　She pat but little faith in:
She gies the herd a pickle nits,　　*shepherd; few*
　　An' twa red-cheekit apples,
To watch, while for the barn she sets,
　　In hopes to see Tam Kipples
　　　　　　That vera night.

22

She turns the key wi' cannie thraw,   *twist*
   An' owre the threshold ventures;
But first on Sawnie gies a ca',
   Syne bauldly in she enters:
A ratton rattl'd up the wa',   *rat*
   An' she cry'd, L--d preserve her!
An' ran thro' midden-hole an' a',
   An' pray'd wi' zeal and fervour
           Fu' fast that night.

23

They hoy't out Will, wi' sair advice;   *urged*
   They hecht him some fine braw ane;   *promised*
It chanc'd the stack he faddom't thrice,
   Was timmer-propt for thrawin: *against bending*
He taks a swirlie, auld moss-oak   *twisted*
   For some black gruesome carlin;   *hag*
An' loot a winze, an' drew a stroke,   *uttered a curse,*
   Till skin in blypes cam haurlin   *and made a hit*
Aff 's nieves that night.   *shreds*
                Off his fists

24

A wanton widow Leezie was,
   As cantie as a kittlin;   *lively; kitten*
But och! that night, amang the shaws,
   She gat a fearfu' settlin!   *woods*
She thro' the whins, an' by the cairn,
   An' owre the hill gaed scrievin;   *careering*
Whare three lairds' lands met at a burn,   *brook*
   To dip her left sark-sleeve in
           Was bent that night.

25

Now; fall	Whyles owre a lin the burnie plays,
	As thro' the glen it wimpl't;
cliff	Whyles round a rocky scaur it strays,
eddy	Whyles in a wiel it dimpl't;
	Whyles glitter'd to the nightly rays,
	Wi' bickerin, dancin dazzle;
hid	Whyles cookit underneath the braes,
	Below the spreading hazel
	Unseen that night.

26

ferns; hillside	Amang the brachens, on the brae,
	Between her an' the moon,
young cow in the open	The Deil, or else an outler quey,
	Gat up an' gae a croon:
leaped; sheath	Poor Leezie's heart maist lap the hool;
lark-high	Near lav'rock-height she jumpit,
foot	But mist a fit, an' in the pool
ears	Out-owre the lugs she plumpit
	Wi' a plunge that night.

27

	In order, on the clean hearth-stane,
	The luggies three are ranged;
	And ev'ry time great care is taen
	To see them duly changed:
1715	Auld uncle John, wha wedlock's joys
	Sin Mar's-year did desire,
empty	Because he gat the toom dish thrice,
	He hav'd them on the fire
	In wrath that night.

28

Wi' merry sangs, an' friendly cracks,
   I wat they did na weary;   *wot*
An unco tales, an' funnie jokes –   *wondrous*
   Their sports were cheap an' cheery:
Till butter'd sow'ns, wi' fragrant lunt,   *steam*
   Set a' their gabs a-steerin;   *tongues wagging*
Syne, wi' a social glass o' strunt,   *liquor*
   They parted aff careerin
          Fu' blythe that night.

Epistle to a Young Friend

1

I lang hae thought, my youthfu' friend,
   A something to have sent you,
Tho' it should serve nae ither end
   Than just a kind memento:
But how the subject-theme may gang,
   Let time and chance determine:
Perhaps it may turn out a sang;
   Perhaps, turn out a sermon.

2

Ye'll try the world soon, my lad;
   And, Andrew dear, believe me,
Ye'll find mankind an unco squad,   *strange*

And muckle they may grieve ye:
   For care and trouble set your thought,
Ev'n when your end's attainèd;
   And a' your views may come to nought,
Where ev'ry nerve is strainèd.

3

I'll no say, men are villains a'
   The real, harden'd wicked,
Wha hae nae check but human law,
   Are to a few restricked;

mighty

But, och! mankind are unco weak
   An' little to be trusted;
If Self the wavering balance shake,
   It's rarely right adjusted!

4

Yet they wha fa' in fortune's strife,
   Their fate we should na censure;
For still, th' important end of life
   They equally may answer:

poverty

A man may hae an honest heart,
   Tho' poortith hourly stare him;
A man may tak a neebor's part,
   Yet hae nae cash to spare him.

5

Ay free, aff han', your story tell,
   When wi' a bosom cronie:
But still keep something to yoursel
   Ye scarcely tell to onie:
Conceal yoursel as weel's ye can

Frae critical dissection:
But keek thro' ev'ry other man   *pry*
   Wi' sharpen'd, sly inspection.

6

The sacred lowe o' weel-plac'd love,   *flame*
   Luxuriantly indulge it;
But never tempt th' illicit rove,   *attempt*
   Tho' naething should divulge it:
I waive the quantum o' the sin,
   The hazard of concealing;
But, och! it hardens a' within,
   And petrifies the feeling!

7

To catch Dame Fortune's golden smile,
   Assiduous wait upon her;
And gather gear by ev'ry wile
   That justify'd by honor:
Not for to hide it in a hedge,
   Nor for a train-attendant;
But for the glorious privilege
   Of being independent.

8

The fear o' Hell's a hangman's whip
   To haud the wretch in order;
But where ye feel your honour grip,
   Let that ay be your border:
Its slightest touches, instant pause –
   Debar a' side-pretences;

An resolutely keep its laws,
  Uncaring consequences.

9

The great Creator to revere
  Must sure become the creature;
But still the preaching cant forbear,
  And ev'n the rigid feature:
Yet ne'er with wits profane to range
  Be complaisance extended;
An atheist-laugh's a poor exchange
  For Deity offended!

10

frolicking

When ranting round in Pleasure's ring,
  Religion may be blinded;
Or if she gie a random sting,
  It may be little minded;
But when on Life we're tempest-driv'n –
  A conscience but a canker –
A correspondence fix'd wi' Heav'n
  Is sure a noble anchor!

11

Adieu, dear, amiable youth!
  Your heart can ne'er be wanting!
May prudence, fortitude, and truth,
  Erect your brow undaunting!
In ploughman phrase, 'God send you speed,'
  Still daily to grow wiser;
heed the council
And may ye better reck the rede,
  Than ever did th' adviser!

On A Scotch Bard

Gone to the West Indies

1

A' ye wha live by sowps o' drink,   *sups*
A' ye wha live by crambo-clink,   *rhyme*
    A' ye wha live and never think,
Come, mourn wi' me!
Our billie 's gien us a' jink,   *comrade; given us*
        An' owre the sea!   *all the slip*

2

Lament him a' ye rantin core,   *jovial set frolic*
Wha dearly like a random-splore;
Nae mair he'll join the merry roar
    In social key;
For now he's taen anither shore,
An' owre the sea!

3

The bonie lasses weel may wiss him,   *wish*
And in their dear petitions place him:
The widows, wives, an' a' may bless him
    Wi' tearfu' e'e,
For weel I wat they'll sairly miss him   *wot*
    That's owre the sea!

4

O Fortune, they hae room to grumble!
Hadst thou taen off some drowsy bummle,   *drone*
Wha can do nought but fyke an' fumble,   *fuss*

'Twad been nae plea;

nimble; wimble   But he was gleg as onie wumble,

That's owre the sea!

5

cheerful   Auld, cantie Kyle may weepers wear,

An' stain them wi' the saut, saut tear:

'Twill mak her poor auld heart, I fear,

splinters   In flinders flee:

He was her Laureat monie a year,

That's owre the sea!

6

He saw Misfortune's cauld nor-west

Lang-mustering up a bitter blast;

jilt   A jillet brak his heart at last,

Ill may she be!

berth   So, took a birth afore the mast,

An' owre the sea.

7

rod   To tremble under Fortune's cummock,

meal and water   On scarce a bellyfu' o' drummock,

Wi' his proud, independent stomach,

Could ill agree;

rolled; buttocks   So, row't his hurdies in a hammock,

An' owre the sea.

8

He ne'er was gien to great misguiding,

pockets   Yet coin his pouches wad na bide in;

Wi' him it ne'er was under hiding,

He dealt it free:

227

The Muse was a' that he took pride in,
    That's owre the sea.

9

Jamaica bodies, use him weel,
An' hap him in a cozie biel: shelter; place
Ye'll find him ay a dainty chiel,
    An' fou o' glee:
He wad na wrang'd the vera Deil,   would not have
    That's owre the sea.

10

Fareweel, my rhyme-composing billie!
Your native soil was right ill-willie;   unkind
But may ye flourish like a lily,
    Now bonilie!
I'll toast you in my hindmost gillie,   last gill
    Tho' owre the sea!

A Dedication

To Gavin Hamilton, Esq

Expect na, sir, in this narration,
A fleechin, fleth'rin Dedication,   wheedling, flattering
To roose you up, an' ca' you guid,   praise
An' sprung o' great an' noble bluid,
Because ye're surnam'd like His Grace,
Perhaps related to the race:

Then, when I'm tired – and sae are ye,
Wi' monie a fulsome, sinfu' lie –
Set up a face how I stop short,
For fear your modesty be hurt.

This may do – maun do, sir, wi' them wha
Maun please the great-folk for a wamefou';
For me! sae laigh I need na bow,
For, Lord be thankit, I can plough;
And when I downa yoke a naig,
then, Lord be thankit, I can beg;
Sae I shall say, an' that's nae flatt'rin,
It's just sic poet an' sic patron

The Poet, some guid angel help him,
Or else, I fear, some ill ane skelp him!
He may do weel for a' he's done yet,
But only he's no just begun yet.

The Patron (sir, ye maun forgie me;
I winna lie, come what will o' me),
On ev'ry hand it will allow'd be,
He's just – nae better than he should be.

I readily and freely grant,
He downa see a poor man want;
What's no his ain he winna tak it;
What ance he says, he winna break it;
Ought he can lend he'll no refus't,
Till aft his guidness is abus'd;
And rascals whyles that do him wrang,
Ev'n that, he does na mind it lang;

bellyful
low

cannot

trounce

sometimes

As master, landlord, husband, father,
He does na fail his part in either.

But then, nae thanks to him for a' that
Nae godly sympton ye can ca' that;
It's naething but a milder feature
Of our poor, sinfu', corrupt nature:
Ye'll get the best o' moral works,
'Mang black Gentoos, and pagan Turks,
Or hunters wild on Ponotaxi,
Wha never heard of orthodoxy.

That he's the poor man's friend in need,
The gentleman in word and deed,
It's no thro' terror of damnation:
It's just a carnal inclination,
And och! that's nae regeneration.

Morality, thou deadly bane,
Thy tens o' thousands thou has slain!
Vain is his hope, whase stay an' trust is
In moral mercy, truth, and justice!

No – stretch a point to catch a plack;   *farthing*
Abuse a brother to his back;
Steal tho' the winnock frae a whore,   *window*
But point the rake that taks the door;
Be to the poor like onie whunstane,
And haud their noses to the grunstane;   *grindstone*
Ply ev'ry art o' legal thieving;
No matter – stick to sound believing.

Learn three-mile pray'rs, an' half-mile graces,

palms

Wi' weel-spread looves, an' lang, wry faces;
Grunt up a solemn, lengthen'd groan,
And damn a' parties but your own;
I'll warrant then, ye're nae deceiver,
A steady, sturdy, staunch believer.

O ye wha leave the springs o' Calvin,

muddy puddles

For gumlie dubs of your ain delvin!
Ye sons of Heresy and Error,
Ye'll some day squeel in quaking terror,
When Vengeance draws the sword in wrath,
And in the fire throws the sheath;
When Ruin, with his sweeping besom,
Just frets till Heav'n commission gies him;
While o'er the harp pale Misery moans,
And strikes the ever-deep'ning tones,
Still louder shrieks, and heavier groans!

Your pardon, sir, for this digression:

almost

I maist forgat my Dedication;
But when divinity comes 'cross me,
My readers still are sure to lose me.

mad

So, Sir, you see 'twas nae daft vapour;
But I maturely thought it proper,
When a' my works I did review,
To dedicate them, Sir, to you:
Because (ye need na tak' it ill),
I thought them something like yoursel.

Then patronize them wi' your favor
And your petitioner shall ever –
I had amaist said, ever pray,
But that's a word I need na say;
For prayin, I hae little skill o't,   *extremely reluctant; bad at it*
I'm baith dead-sweer, an' wretched ill o't;
But I'se repeat each poor man's pray'r,   *I'll*
That kens or hears about you, Sir:–

May ne'er Misfortune's gowling bark
Howl thro' the dwelling o' the clerk!   *lawyer*
May ne'er his gen'rous, honest heart,
For that same gen'rous spirit smart!
May Kennedy's far-honor'd name
Lang beet his hymeneal flame,   *feed*
Till Hamiltons, at least a dizzen,
Are frae their nuptial labors risen:
Five bonie lasses round their table,
And sev'n braw fellows, stout an' able,
To serve their king an' country weel,
By word, or pen, or pointed steel!
May Health and Peace, with mutual rays,
Shine on the ev'ning o' his days;
Till his wee, curlie John's ier-oe,   *great-grandchild*
When ebbing life nae mair shall flow,
The last, sad, mournful rites bestow!'

I will not wind a lang conclusion
With complimentary effusion;
But, whilst your wishes and endeavours
Are blest with Fortune's smiles and favours,

I am, dear sir, with zeal most fervent,
Your much indebted, humble servant.
　　But if (which Pow'rs above prevent)
That iron-hearted carl, Want,
Attended, in his grim advances,
By sad mistakes, and black mischances,
While hopes, and joys, and pleasures fly him,
Make you as poor a dog as I am,
Your 'humble servant' then no more;
For who would humbly serve the poor?
But, by a poor man's hopes in Heav'n!
While recollection's pow'r is giv'n,
If, in the vale of humble life,
The victim sad of Fortune's strife,
I, thro' the tender-gushing tear,
Should recognise my master dear;
If friendless, low, we meet together,
Then, sir, your hand – my FRIEND and
　　　　BROTHER!

Index of Titles

COLLINS

Other Scottish-interest titles include:

Gem Whisky
The essential guide to over 150 Scotch whiskies
and the distilleries that produce them **£3.99**

Gem Clans and Tartans
Over 100 Scottish tartans illustrated in colour,
with histories of their clans **£3.99**

Gem Burns Anthology
A pocket-sized anthology of the best songs and
poetry of Scotland's national poet **£3.99**

Gem Famous Scots
An essential guide to over 150 prominent
Scottish men and women of the past and
present **£3.99**

Pocket Reference Scotland
A fully illustrated guide with many maps and
cultural and practical information **£5.99**

Collins Touring Guide to Scotland
Scotland's landscape and history captured in
colour photographs and informative text **£6.99**

Index of First Lines